DIAGNOSING AND TREATING MENTAL ILLNESS

GENERAL EDITORS

Dale C. Garell, M.D.
Medical Director, California Children Services, Department of Health
    Services, County of Los Angeles
Associate Dean for Curriculum
Clinical Professor, Department of Pediatrics & Family Medicine,
    University of Southern California School of Medicine
Former President, Society for Adolescent Medicine

Solomon H. Snyder, M.D.
Distinguished Service Professor of Neuroscience, Pharmacology, and
    Psychiatry, Johns Hopkins University School of Medicine
Former president, Society of Neuroscience
Albert Lasker Award in Medical Research, 1978

CONSULTING EDITORS

Robert W. Blum, M.D., Ph.D.
Associate Professor, School of Public Health and Department of
    Pediatrics
Director, Adolescent Health Program, University of Minnesota
Consultant, World Health Organization

Charles E. Irwin, Jr., M.D.
Associate Professor of Pediatrics; Director, Division of Adolescent
    Medicine, University of California, San Francisco

Lloyd J. Kolbe, Ph.D.
Chief, Office of School Health & Special Projects, Center for Health
    Promotion & Education, Centers for Disease Control
President, American School Health Association

Jordan J. Popkin
Director, Division of Federal Employee Occupational Health, U.S. Public
    Health Service Region I

Joseph L. Rauh, M.D.
Professor of Pediatrics and Medicine, Adolescent Medicine, Children's
    Hospital Medical Center, Cincinnati
Former president, Society for Adolescent Medicine

THE ENCYCLOPEDIA OF
H E A L T H

PSYCHOLOGICAL DISORDERS
AND THEIR TREATMENT

Solomon H. Snyder, M.D. · General Editor

DIAGNOSING AND TREATING MENTAL ILLNESS

Allan Lundy

Introduction by C. Everett Koop, M.D., Sc.D.
former Surgeon General, U.S. Public Health Service

CHELSEA HOUSE PUBLISHERS
New York · Philadelphia

The goal of the ENCYCLOPEDIA OF HEALTH is to provide general information in the ever-changing areas of physiology, psychology, and related medical issues. The titles in this series are not intended to take the place of the professional advice of a physician or other health-care professional.

ON THE COVER *Hell in My Head* by Andrzej Dudzinski
Chelsea House Publishers
EDITOR-IN-CHIEF Nancy Toff
EXECUTIVE EDITOR Remmel T. Nunn
MANAGING EDITOR Karyn Gullen Browne
COPY CHIEF Juliann Barbato
PICTURE EDITOR Adrian G. Allen
ART DIRECTOR Maria Epes
MANUFACTURING MANAGER Gerald Levine

The Encyclopedia of Health
SENIOR EDITOR Paula Edelson

Staff for DIAGNOSING AND TREATING MENTAL ILLNESS
ASSISTANT EDITOR Laura Dolce
COPY EDITOR Richard Klin
EDITORIAL ASSISTANTS Leigh Hope Wood
PICTURE RESEARCHER Villette Harris
ASSISTANT ART DIRECTOR Loraine Machlin
SENIOR DESIGNER Marjorie Zaum
DESIGN ASSISTANT Debora Smith
PRODUCTION MANAGER Joseph Romano
PRODUCTION COORDINATOR Marie Claire Cebrián

First Printing

1 3 5 7 9 8 6 4 2

Library of Congress Cataloging-in-Publication Data

Lundy, Allan.
   Diagnosing and treating mental illness/Allan Lundy;
introduction by C. Everett Koop.
      p. cm.—(The Encyclopedia of health. Psychological disorders and their treatment)
   Includes bibliographical references.
   Summary: Discusses the types of mental illness and describes how they are diagnosed and treated.
   ISBN 0-7910-0047-8
        0-7910-0513-5 (pbk.)
   1. Mental illness—Juvenile literature.   2. Psychiatry—Juvenile literature.
3. Psychotherapy—Juvenile literature.   [1. Mental illness.   2. Psychotherapy.
3. Psychiatry.]   I. Title.   II. Series.   89-22119
RC460.2.L86 1990   CIP
616.89—dc19   AC

CONTENTS

PREVENTION AND EDUCATION: THE KEYS TO GOOD HEALTH

C. Everett Koop, M.D., Sc.D.
former Surgeon General,
U.S. Public Health Service

The issue of health education has received particular attention in recent years because of the presence of AIDS in the news. But our response to this particular tragedy points up a number of broader issues that doctors, public health officials, educators, and the public face. In particular, it points up the necessity for sound health education for citizens of all ages.

Over the past 25 years this country has been able to bring about dramatic declines in the death rates for heart disease, stroke, accidents, and, for people under the age of 45, cancer. Today, Americans generally eat better and take better care of themselves than ever before. Thus, with the help of modern science and technology, they have a better chance of surviving serious—even catastrophic—illnesses. That's the good news.

But, like every phonograph record, there's a flip side, and one with special significance for young adults. According to a report issued in 1979 by Dr. Julius Richmond, my predecessor as Surgeon General, Americans aged 15 to 24 had a higher death rate in 1979 than they did 20 years earlier. The causes: violent death and injury, alcohol and drug abuse, unwanted pregnancies, and sexually transmitted diseases. Adolescents are particularly vulnerable, because they are beginning to explore their own sexuality and perhaps to experiment with drugs. The need for educating young people is critical, and the price of neglect is high.

Yet even for the population as a whole, our health is still far from what it could be. Why? A 1974 Canadian government report attributed all death and disease to four broad elements: inadequacies in the health-care system, behavioral factors or unhealthy life-styles, environmental hazards, and human biological factors.

To be sure, there are diseases that are still beyond the control of even our advanced medical knowledge and techniques. And despite yearnings that are as old as the human race itself, there is no "fountain of youth" to ward off aging and death. Still, there is a solution to many of the problems that undermine sound health. In a word, that solution is prevention. Prevention, which includes health promotion and education, saves lives, improves the quality of life, and, in the long run, saves money.

In the United States, organized public health activities and preventive medicine have a long history. Important milestones include the improvement of sanitary procedures and the development of pasteurized milk in the late 19th century, and the introduction in the mid-20th century of effective vaccines against polio, measles, German measles, mumps, and other once-rampant diseases. Internationally, organized public health efforts began on a wide-scale basis with the International Sanitary Conference of 1851, to which 12 nations sent representatives. The World Health Organization, founded in 1948, continues these efforts under the aegis of the United Nations, with particular emphasis on combatting communicable diseases and the training of health-care workers.

But despite these accomplishments, much remains to be done in the field of prevention. For too long, we have had a medical care system that is science- and technology-based, focused, essentially, on illness and mortality. It is now patently obvious that both the social and the economic costs of such a system are becoming insupportable.

Implementing prevention—and its corollaries, health education and promotion—is the job of several groups of people:

First, the medical and scientific professions need to continue basic scientific research, and here we are making considerable progress. But increased concern with prevention will also have a decided impact on how primary-care doctors practice medicine. With a shift to health-based rather than morbidity-based medicine, the role of the "new physician" will include a healthy dose of patient education.

Second, practitioners of the social and behavioral sciences—psychologists, economists, city planners—along with lawyers, business leaders, and government officials—must solve the practical and ethical dilemmas confronting us: poverty, crime, civil rights, literacy, education, employment, housing, sanitation, environmental protection, health care delivery systems, and so forth. All of these issues affect public health.

Third is the public at large. We'll consider that very important group in a moment.

Fourth, and the linchpin in this effort, is the public health profession—doctors, epidemiologists, teachers—who must harness the professional expertise of the first two groups and the common sense and cooperation of the third, the public. They must define the problems statistically and qualitatively and then help us set priorities for finding the solutions.

To a very large extent, improving those statistics is the responsibility of every individual. So let's consider more specifically what the role of the individual should be and why health education is so important to that role. First, and most obviously, individuals can protect themselves from illness and injury and thus minimize their need for professional medical care. They can eat a nutritious diet, get adequate exercise, avoid tobacco, alcohol, and drugs, and take prudent steps to avoid accidents. The proverbial "apple a day keeps the doctor away" is not so far from the truth, after all.

Second, individuals should actively participate in their own medical care. They should schedule regular medical and dental checkups. Should they develop an illness or injury, they should know when to treat themselves and when to seek professional help. To gain the maximum benefit from any medical treatment that they do require, individuals must become partners in that treatment. For instance, they should understand the effects and side effects of medications. I counsel young physicians that there is no such thing as too much information when talking with patients. But the corollary is the patient must know enough about the nuts and bolts of the healing process to understand what the doctor is telling him. That is at least partially the patient's responsibility.

Education is equally necessary for us to understand the ethical and public policy issues in health care today. Sometimes individuals will encounter these issues in making decisions about their own treatment or that of family members. Other citizens may encounter them as jurors in medical malpractice cases. But we all become involved, indirectly, when we elect our public officials, from school board members to the president. Should surrogate parenting be legal? To what extent is drug testing desirable, legal, or necessary? Should there be public funding for family planning, hospitals, various types of medical research, and medical care for the indigent? How should we allocate scant technological resources, such as kidney dialysis and organ transplants? What is the proper role of government in protecting the rights of patients?

What are the broad goals of public health in the United States today? In 1980, the Public Health Service issued a report aptly entitled *Promoting Health-Preventing Disease: Objectives for the Nation.*This report expressed its goals in terms of mortality and in terms of intermediate goals in education and health improvement. It identified 15 major concerns: controlling high blood pressure; improving family planning; improving pregnancy care and infant health; increasing the rate of immunization; controlling sexually transmitted diseases; controlling the presence of toxic agents and radiation in the environment; improving occupational safety and health; preventing accidents; promoting water fluoridation and dental health; controlling infectious diseases; decreasing smoking; decreasing alcohol and drug abuse; improving nutrition; promoting physical fitness and exercise; and controlling stress and violent behavior.

For healthy adolescents and young adults (ages 15 to 24), the specific goal was a 20% reduction in deaths, with a special focus on motor vehicle injuries and alcohol and drug abuse. For adults (ages 25 to 64), the aim was 25% fewer deaths, with a concentration on heart attacks, strokes, and cancers.

Smoking is perhaps the best example of how individual behavior can have a direct impact on health. Today cigarette smoking is recognized as the most important single preventable cause of death in our society. It is responsible for more cancers and more cancer deaths than any other known agent; is a prime risk factor for heart and blood vessel disease, chronic bronchitis, and emphysema; and is a frequent cause of complications in pregnancies and of babies born prematurely, underweight, or with potentially fatal respiratory and cardiovascular problems.

Since the release of the Surgeon General's first report on smoking in 1964, the proportion of adult smokers has declined substantially, from 43% in 1965 to 30.5% in 1985. Since 1965, 37 million people have quit smoking. Although there is still much work to be done if we are to become a "smoke-free society," it is heartening to note that public health and public education efforts—such as warnings on cigarette packages and bans on broadcast advertising—have already had significant effects.

In 1835, Alexis de Tocqueville, a French visitor to America, wrote, "In America the passion for physical well-being is general." Today, as then, health and fitness are front-page items. But with the greater scientific and technological resources now available to us, we are in a far stronger position to make good health care available to everyone. And with the greater technological threats to us as we approach the 21st century, the need to do so is more urgent than ever before. Comprehensive information about basic biology, preventive medicine, medical and surgical treatments, and related ethical and public policy issues can help you arm yourself with the knowledge you need to be healthy throughout your life.

FOREWORD

Solomon H. Snyder, M.D.

Mental disorders represent the number one health problem for the United States and probably for the entire human population. Some studies estimate that approximately one-third of all Americans suffer from some sort of emotional disturbance. Depression of varying severity will affect as many as 20 percent of all of us at one time or another in our lives. Severe anxiety is even more common.

Adolescence is a time of particular susceptibility to emotional problems. Teenagers are undergoing significant changes in their brain as well as their physical structure. The hormones that alter the organs of reproduction during puberty also influence the way we think and feel. At a purely psychological level, adolescents must cope with major upheavals in their lives. After years of not noticing the opposite sex, they find themselves romantically attracted but must painfully learn the skills of social interchange both for superficial, flirtatious relationships and for genuine intimacy. Teenagers must develop new ways of relating to their parents. Adolescents strive for independence. Yet, our society is structured in such a way that teenagers must remain dependent on their parents for many more years. During adolescence, young men and women examine their own intellectual bents and begin to plan the type of higher education and vocation they believe they will find most fulfilling.

Because of all these challenges, teenagers are more emotionally volatile than adults. Passages from extreme exuberance to dejection are common. The emotional distress of completely normal adolescence can be so severe that the same disability in an adult would be labeled as major mental illness. Although most teenagers somehow muddle through and emerge unscathed, a number of problems are more frequent among adolescents than among adults. Many psychological aberrations reflect severe disturbances, although these are sometimes not regarded as "psychiatric." Eating disorders, to which young adults are especially vulnerable, are an example. An extremely large number of teenagers diet to great excess even though they are not overweight. Many of them suffer from a specific disturbance referred to as anorexia nervosa, a form of self-starvation that is just as real a disorder as diabetes. The same is true for those who eat compulsively and then sometimes force themselves to vomit. They may be afflicted with bulimia.

Depression is also surprisingly frequent among adolescents, although its symptoms may be less obvious in young people than they are in adults. And, because suicide occurs most frequently in those suffering from depression, we must be on the lookout for subtle hints of despondency in those close to us. This is especially urgent because teenage suicide is a rapidly worsening national problem.

The volumes on Psychological Disorders and Their Treatment in the ENCYCLOPEDIA OF HEALTH cover the major areas of mental illness, from mild to severe. They also emphasize the means available for getting help. *Anxiety and Phobias, Depression,* and *Schizophrenia* deal specifically with these forms of mental disturbance. *Child Abuse* and *Delinquency and Criminal Behavior* explore abnormalities of behavior that may stem from environmental and social influences as much as from biological or psychological illness. *Personality Disorders* and *Compulsive Behavior* explain how people develop disturbances of their overall personality. *Learning Disabilities* investigates disturbances of the mind that may reflect neurological derangements as much as psychological abnormalities. *Mental Retardation* explains the various causes of this many-sided handicap, including the genetic component, complications during pregnancy, and traumas during birth. *Suicide* discusses the epidemiology of this tragic phenomenon and outlines the assistance available to those who are at risk. *Stress Management* locates the sources of stress in contemporary society and considers formal strategies for coping with it. Finally, *Diagnosing and Treating Mental Illness* explains to the reader how professionals sift through various signs and symptoms to define the exact nature of the various mental disorders and fully describes the most effective means of alleviating them.

Fortunately, when it comes to psychological disorders, knowing the facts is a giant step toward solving the problems.

CHAPTER 1

A SEARCH FOR UNDERSTANDING

A 16th-century painting of an exorcism.

Since the beginning of civilization, people have attempted to understand the causes of human emotional behavior. Most primitive societies believed that mental illnesses were caused by a demon who took possession of the victim's body. The early Greeks, Chinese, Hebrews, and Egyptians all treated mental disturbances with "exorcisms"—ritual acts consisting of prayers, flogging, starvation, and drugs to induce vomiting. The purpose of the exorcism was to make the body so uncomfortable that the demon would want to leave.

The rise of Greek civilization around 900 B.C. saw the first rational and scientific explanations of mental disturbances. The Greek physician Hippocrates proposed a remarkably insightful theory of the causes of mental illness. He believed that abnormal behavior resulted mainly from brain injury or disease, with some influence from heredity and social stresses. Treatments prescribed by the ancient Greeks and Romans were often badly misguided, however. For example, they believed that certain illnesses were caused by an excess of blood in the body, so they would attach leeches (bloodsucking parasites) to the patient to drain the excess blood.

Superstition returned when the collapse of the Roman Empire in A.D. 476 brought on the Dark Ages, which lasted until about the year 1000. Although the ancient rational explanations survived in the Arab world, the rest of Europe accepted the Christian dogma that illness was a punishment from God.

By the 14th and 15th centuries, the bubonic plague (a tremendously contagious disease caused by a bacterium) had killed off nearly three-quarters of the population, and the social structure of Europe was crumbling. In an effort to maintain their authority, Church leaders blamed supernatural forces for the terrible events. In 1484, Pope Innocent VIII issued a decree directing the clergy to find and execute witches. The victims of this persecution, which lasted for centuries, were frequently those who exhibited odd or disturbing behavior. The mentally ill who escaped the witch hunts were generally either locked away by their relatives or abandoned to wander and beg.

Still, humane voices could sometimes be heard even in the Middle Ages. As early as the 14th century, the Belgian town of Gheel became a haven for the mentally ill because of the martyrdom of Saint Dyphna there. According to legend, Dyphna's father, an Irish king, went mad with grief at the death of his wife and proposed marriage to his daughter. The horrified girl fled to Belgium, where she was found at Gheel and beheaded by her insane father. Later, 10 "lunatics" were reported to have been miraculously cured there, and Dyphna became the patron saint of the mentally ill. The townspeople of Gheel began to take in and care for the afflicted, a tradition that continues to this day.

In addition, there were those who believed that bizarre behavior was not caused by possession. In 1563 Johannes Weyer,

A mania for dancing grew widespread in medieval Europe in reaction to the bubonic plague. This disease, which swept through Europe in the 14th and 15th centuries, wiped out nearly two-thirds of the population in some areas.

a courageous German physician sometimes called the first psychiatrist, asserted that many "witches" were actually mentally ill. In his book *De Praestigiis Daemonum* (The Deception of Demons), he wrote tartly that "our expenses would diminish considerably if we put to better use the logs and bundles used to burn innocent people." Weyer also demonstrated that a number of people who claimed to have been bewitched were faking their symptoms. One girl was found to have been secretly fed by her sister, whereas her parents believed she had no food for months.

Gradually, the belief in witchcraft and demonic possession diminished, but the insane were still imprisoned in horrible conditions of filth and brutality. Their harsh treatment continued until the French Revolution of 1789, which brought to Europe a new humanitarian spirit. A shy, studious physician named Philippe Pinel was appointed director of Bicêtre, the Parisian insane asylum. Pinel introduced radical changes. He had the inmates released from their chains, allowed them fresh air and exercise, and directed that they be treated in a kindly manner. The results surprised skeptics who had declared that unchained patients would become violent. The reforms actually led to calmer inmates who recovered more quickly. Pinel's humane approach spread throughout France, making the nation a model of enlightened care for the mentally ill.

THE SEARCH FOR THE CAUSES OF MENTAL ILLNESS

By the late 18th century, most people were convinced that mental disturbances were not caused by supernatural powers. Scientists, however, were still unsure whether such illnesses stemmed from physical malfunctions or psychological abnormalities.

The 19th century saw an explosion of interest in medical theories regarding mental disorders. In 1861, Paul Pierre Broca discovered that tumors or injuries to a particular part of the brain led to speech loss. Perhaps brain damage caused other behavioral

During the Middle Ages the mentally ill were often hunted and persecuted as witches. Many insane people, such as the woman shown here in this 16th-century engraving, were burned alive.

disturbances. But often, the brains of the mentally ill, when dissected, appeared perfectly normal. Then the French chemist Louis Pasteur formulated the germ theory of disease. Pasteur believed that tiny microscopic organisms were responsible for causing many diseases. His theory suggested that such organisms could cause mental disturbances, as well. The idea was supported by the discovery in 1897 that one type of madness, general paresis, resulted from the same microorganism that caused syphilis. Throughout this period, most physicians were convinced that mental illnesses stemmed from brain damage or disease. Today, many researchers still believe that all serious mental disorders will someday be traced to physical causes.

Nevertheless, it is clear that some mental disturbances can be traced to an individual's particular experiences and beliefs. This modern psychological point of view had a curious beginning. In the late 18th century a charismatic German physician named Franz Anton Mesmer developed an eccentric theory. He believed that the planets controlled the flow of a magnetic fluid in the body, which determined mental and physical health. Mesmer redirected his patients' "fluid" into a more healthy flow by means of his own "animal magnetism." No responsible physician believed in Mesmer's theory, even in the 18th century. He was more of a showman than a scientist, but his treatments had an impact on psychology for a good reason: They often worked. Mesmer's technique, called mesmerism, was later refined to hypnotism, a practice of inducing an extremely suggestive mental state in patients through the use of suggestions of the hypnotist.

Hypnosis began to influence theories of mental illness in the 1870s. Jean-Martin Charcot, a brilliant French neurologist, showed that symptoms of hysteria such as paralysis or blindness could be hypnotically induced in normal persons. Hypnotic suggestion could also be used to temporarily alleviate hysterical symptoms. Obviously, hypnosis was not capable of causing or removing brain damage. Charcot and other researchers were forced to conclude that purely emotional experiences were at the root of many mental illnesses. This opened the door for the theories of the Viennese physician Sigmund Freud.

Like others attending medical school in the 1870s, Freud had been taught that mental illnesses had physical causes. After

An 18th-century painting depicts an aide of the physician Philippe Pinel unshackling a patient. Pinel (left of the patient) was the first doctor to recommend humane treatment for the insane.

studying with Charcot, and treating a number of hysterics himself, Freud began to construct his famous psychoanalytic theory. The theory, explained in detail in Chapter 6, proposes that mental disorders arise from emotionally charged childhood events. To pay his way through medical school, Freud had worked for five years as a research biologist. Because of this training, he believed that a person's early development was extremely important for later mental health. He knew that "as the twig is bent, so grows the tree." Imagine two trees, one growing on the rocky, windswept peak of a mountain, the other in a fertile, protected valley. The one on the peak grows up small and stunted, and less likely to survive later storms. Freud applied this theory to human nature.

Freud also believed that the human mind is divided into three categories: the id, the ego, and the superego. The id is the human unconscious, dominated by drives such as sex and aggression. The superego is the internalization of parental and societal rules. The ego, which is roughly equivalent to the conscious mind, serves as a mediator between the other two divisions. Freud's ideas revolutionized psychology and psychiatry and profoundly altered the educated person's concept of human nature.

Of course, many other men and women contributed to scientific knowledge of mental processes and the causes of abnormal behavior. Besides the psychoanalysts who made suggested revisions of Freud's theory, a number of therapists developed strikingly different concepts of the causes of human behavior. Like Freud, the American psychologist Carl Rogers believed that emotional disorders have their origins in childhood. But he felt that they were caused by parents who put conditions on their love for the child. On the other hand, Albert Ellis, another American, felt unhappiness was the result of illogical thinking. Ellis believed that if a person could recognize his or her own mistaken beliefs, he or she could stop feeling miserable.

A group of researchers called behaviorists, such as the American psychologist B. F. Skinner, believe that emotional and mental disorders are little more than bad habits. They have shown

French neurologist Jean-Martin Charcot demonstrated that certain symptoms of hysteria, such as blindness and paralysis, could be hypnotically induced.

that people can be taught to replace abnormal behaviors with normal ones simply by controlling rewards and punishments.

Finally, many medical researchers have contributed to the latest, most exciting development in the treatment of disorders: drug therapy. New psychoactive drugs have alleviated the suffering of millions and suggest that true cures of mental disturbances may be possible by altering the patient's brain chemistry.

The debate over the relative importance of physical versus psychological causes of mental illness continues. Most therapists now believe, however, that the profoundly abnormal behaviors of psychosis have mainly physical causes. The less severe anxiety disorders probably have their origin in past experience.

Nothing in the universe is so complex as the human mind. It is not surprising, then, that it should sometimes malfunction. The following chapters will explore different types of mental disturbances, the ways clinicians diagnose patient disorders, and the many forms of therapy available to help correct disorders.

• • • •

CHAPTER 2

THE TYPES OF MENTAL DISTURBANCES

It happens several times a day in a big-city hospital. The police have brought in a man who seems confused, mumbling incoherently. He is filthy. But he has been brought to the hospital not because of his mental condition but because he has fallen and cut his head. Is he psychotic, perhaps a schizophrenic or manic-depressive? Or a drug abuser? Or did the blow to his head cause his disturbed behavior?

In a very different setting, a teenager hesitantly approaches the office of the school counselor. She knows there is something wrong with her thinking. For weeks, she has been tense, tired, unable to concentrate. Floating through her mind are odd images of death: in a car crash, by mistaking a bottle of bleach for a bottle of milk, or from a horrible disease in which her insides have turned to maggots. But her doctor has told her there is no physical problem.

In both these cases, what is required is a diagnosis, a labeling of the disturbance. The diagnosis of mental illness is a complex and difficult matter. The symptoms of a particular mental disturbance can be obvious or subtle, can be present one day and gone the next, and can easily be confused with those of other illnesses.

Still, diagnosis has proven to be worth the effort for the therapist. A careful diagnosis aids treatment in several ways. First, it helps the therapist organize and summarize what he or she knows about the patient's disturbance. Second, it suggests particular treatment approaches that other therapists have found effective for the same problem. Third, it aids in accurate prognosis—the prediction of the future course of the disease.

A standardized diagnosis is also useful in communicating information. When researchers publish the results of their studies, their readers share the same definitions of important terms. Schools, courts, and insurance companies may need an objective description of the disturbance for their records. And when therapy is conducted by several different persons, as in a large psychiatric hospital, the diagnosis provides a quick summary of the patient's disturbance.

Traditionally, most specific disorders have been grouped into three broad categories of mental disturbances. These are the psychoses, the neuroses, and the personality disorders.

In contrast to these broad categories of mental disorders, the determination of insanity is not a psychiatric diagnosis but strictly a legal term. According to the law, insanity means mental derangement that makes a person incapable of rational conduct or judgment. Many psychotics and a few neurotics would probably be found insane by a court hearing.

The authoritative guide to the classification of mental illness is the American Psychiatric Association's *Diagnostic and Statistical Manual of Mental Disorders, Third Edition*, Revised, known as the DSM-IIIR. This guide sets out the symptoms and behaviors typical of a wide variety of mental disturbances, both major and minor. In the following sections the most common disorders will be outlined, as well as some of the best treatments for them, especially when treatments other than psychotherapy seem most effective.

THE PSYCHOTIC DISORDERS

Psychotic disorders are the most serious type of mental illness, for they can involve a complete break with reality. Psychotics cannot distinguish between what is really happening and what is occurring only in their mind.

Schizophrenia

Schizophrenia strikes about 1% of all Americans. It is the most disabling and the most frightening of all the mental illnesses. No other disorder strikes so devastatingly at the core of a person's personality. Schizophrenia is a disorder of thinking: Thought processes are jumbled, illogical, and bizarre. The following is a response given by a schizophrenic when asked why he was in the hospital for treatment:

> I'm a cut donator, donated by double sacrifice. I get two days for every one. That's known as double sacrifice; in other words, standard cut donator. You know, we considered it. He couldn't have anything for the cut, or for these patients.

A schizophrenic often has delusions, or false beliefs that logic or contrary evidence cannot shake. Common delusions include the belief that the victim's body is rotting away or that his thoughts are being broadcast for all to hear or are being controlled by outside forces. Some schizophrenics also suffer from what are called "delusions of reference." These delusions occur when the schizophrenic interprets ordinary events as having a special significance for himself or herself alone. One might believe, for example, that a glance from a passing stranger is an order from outer space to prepare the planet for invasion.

Hallucinations, or false sensory perceptions, are also common. The International Pilot Study of Schizophrenia, compiled by the World Health Organization in 1973, examined nine countries as diverse as Denmark, Nigeria, the United States, and the USSR. It indicated that 70% of all schizophrenics experience hallucinations in which they hear voices. Finally, a common symptom of the illness is "flattened affect," or a leveling of the normal peaks and valleys of emotion. A schizophrenic might describe her father's death, for example, with no trace of emotion at all.

For all the research being done on schizophrenia, many people misunderstand what it is. Schizophrenia is not a split personality, a rare disorder depicted in such books and films as *Sybil* or *The Three Faces of Eve*. People have confused the two disturbances because the word "schizophrenia" literally means "split mind." However, with schizophrenia, the "split" might better be thought of as a splintering or shattering—the mind works in fragments that have lost their logical connections.

The DSM-IIIR specifies that a person is schizophrenic if he or she has bizarre delusions or hears voices occurring frequently for at least a week. This disorder is also diagnosed when, for a

Catatonic schizophrenics, such as the woman shown here, hold bodily postures for long periods of time.

week or more, there is a combination of less extreme symptoms. These combinations might include flattened affect along with incoherent speech or less illogical delusions combined with hallucinations that do not include voices.

A diagnosis of schizophrenia is based, in addition to the preceding, on the presence of several manifestations. These include the loss of the ability to perform everyday activities such as studying or keeping clean and a history of at least six months of lesser symptoms of psychosis. Social isolation, peculiar behavior such as collecting garbage, vague or strange speech, and inappropriate emotional reactions are some secondary indications. In summary, then, schizophrenia is diagnosed only when one's behavior has been disturbed for at least six months, when a person's behavior prevents him or her from leading a normal life, and when there has been a week or more of truly bizarre activity.

The DSM-IIIR also lists three distinct diagnostic types of schizophrenia. Patients with catatonic schizophrenia express their confusion of thought through bodily postures. This type of schizophrenic might fall into a stupor or adopt a bizarre—often dramatic—pose that he or she will hold for a long time. The patient may burst out into wild, violent physical activity.

Disorganized schizophrenia, as the name implies, is characterized by incoherent or particularly bizarre speech and emotional expressions. Sometimes this type of schizophrenic behaves in a silly, childish manner. A victim of this disease may giggle and stick out her tongue when meeting a stranger.

Paranoid schizophrenia is the most common of the three types. The paranoid schizophrenic may have delusions of grandeur—believing that he or she has special powers, is a superior being, or is a famous historical figure, such as Napoleon or Jesus. The victim may also suffer from delusions of persecution, misinterpreting the innocent deeds of others as threats. He or she may perceive a friendly smile, for example, as a knowing smirk or a cruel sneer.

The task of diagnosing this type of schizophrenia is complicated by the fact that most victims show a mixture of symptoms. One person may express paranoid ideas in jumbled, incoherent speech, for example, whereas another may be hospitalized in a catatonic state on one occasion and develop paranoid symptoms a few months later.

Some doctors have interpreted the triangular forms in this painting by a schizophrenic as the patient's search for stability in his life.

Another useful distinction is between process and reactive schizophrenia. With many forms of schizophrenia, the speed with which the symptoms of the illness develop is closely related to the speed with which they diminish. When the disturbance has had a slow onset beginning in childhood, it is called process schizophrenia. In this case, symptoms tend to leave slowly, and there is little hope for a complete recovery. On the other hand, when symptoms come on very suddenly in adulthood—reactive schizophrenia—prognosis for recovery is very good.

About one-fourth of all schizophrenics eventually recover and resume an essentially normal life. Another 25% deteriorate and must live out their lives in a mental hospital. The rest recover somewhat but are in danger of a relapse. Patients with higher intelligence, or with more stable personalities before becoming psychotic, have a better prognosis.

Treatment for schizophrenia includes drugs to reduce psychotic hallucinations and delusions and behavioral retraining to allow the sufferer to take care of his or her daily needs. Psychotherapy is of little use, perhaps because the patient's thought processes are too confused to benefit from another person's point of view.

Paranoia and Other Psychotic Delusions

Sometimes people have delusions that are not accompanied by the bizarre thinking or hallucinations that indicate schizophrenia. Instead, their delusions take the form of conceivable real-life situations, such as being investigated by the FBI or dying of a terrible disease. Common delusions of this type include irrational jealousy, the belief that another (often famous) person is in love with them, or the belief that one has some special powers, such as being able to communicate with space creatures. In a paranoid delusion, the victim believes that he is being plotted against, that his movements are being watched, and that his ambitions are being thwarted by a conspiracy. Treatment is difficult for patients with a paranoid delusion, for the patient is likely to believe that the therapist is part of the conspiracy against him.

Infantile Autism

Autism, which appears in children almost from birth, is characterized by a profound detachment from other people. Autistic infants may fail to become upset when left alone, and will not respond affectionately when picked up. By the age of two or three, autistics may become fascinated by mechanical objects, or they may perform repetitive actions, such as rocking back and forth for hours. Because these children have little desire to communicate with others, their language development is slow and sometimes distorted. The DSM-IIIR cites an example of an autistic child who, when hurt, would cry out, "Cheese, cheese, cheese."

In adulthood, the autistic person still has little interest in any sort of human contact and thus possesses very poor social skills. One autistic adult believed that all other humans except himself could read minds; this was the only way he could explain the normal human ability to empathize with others and to predict their reactions. For him, it was a mystery why people laugh at a joke, get angry at an insult, or grieve at the death of a friend. Little can be done for the autistic child or adult, beyond attempting to train the victim to live in a world he or she can never fully understand.

Depression

Every person feels sad at some point in his or her life. It is normal to become a bit moody in response to loss or failure. Often these feelings may persist for a week or two, without an obvious cause. These feelings of being "down" are known as depression.

Depression commonly affects people's physical functions. A depressed person often complains of fatigue, listlessness, and constipation. The victim may have difficulty in falling asleep, or may want to sleep all the time. Overeating is common in mild depression, yet a loss of appetite often is a symptom of more severe depression.

Depression, and mania, its opposite, are called affective disorders because they involve disturbances in affect, or mood. Typically, a mildly depressed person feels a loss of energy, sadness, and a lowered sense of self-esteem. But when depression is severe for no apparent reason, or continues for a very long time, it may be diagnosed as a neurotic or even a psychotic disorder.

Usually a depressed person is well aware of his or her depression, and can report accurately on the depth of negative feelings. Sometimes, however, depression hides beneath other symptoms, often the physical disturbances described above. Children and adolescents especially may seem to be hyperactive, irritable, or antisocial, when they are really depressed.

Neurotic depression is diagnosed when the depressed mood continues for a year or more and includes at least two other symptoms, such as poor appetite combined with low self-esteem, or poor concentration with feelings of hopelessness.

A "major depressive episode," according to the DSM-IIIR, is a combination of five or more severe symptoms, all occurring at about the same time. These symptoms include, for example, a constant lack of interest in everyday activities, significant weight loss or gain, extreme restlessness or sluggishness, exaggerated feelings of worthlessness or guilt, and frequent fantasies of suicide. Sometimes a major depressive episode is diagnosed as a "melancholic type" when it includes a lack of ability to feel pleasure when a happy event occurs, when the depression is worse in the morning, and when the victim wakes up each morning at least two hours earlier than usual.

Severe depression may sometimes include the psychotic symptoms of delusions or hallucinations. Delusions of physical deterioration are common. A psychotically depressed person may believe that his or her intestines have turned to slime or his or her brains have turned into sawdust. Hallucinations typically focus on themes of guilt, punishment, or death.

Sometimes periods of depression alternate with their opposite, an illness known as mania. A manic (not to be confused with maniac) has tremendous energy, a great appetite for work or special projects, little need for sleep, lowered inhibitions, and often suffers from delusions of grandeur. Usually, after a few days or weeks in the manic state, the exhausted victim gradually slips back into depression. Some psychiatrists believe that depression in these patients, the "bipolar" group, is different from depression in those who have never had a manic period. Manic-depressives may have had better family situations and appear to respond better to certain drugs than those in the "unipolar," or depression-only, group.

Treatment for depression has been revolutionized by the discovery of tricyclic antidepressants. These drugs have probably saved more lives than any other psychoactive medications because they help alleviate suicidal impulses.

Suicide is a very real danger for people who are severely depressed; 15% to 20% take their own lives. Although it is commonly assumed that a person who talks about suicide will not really attempt it, this is simply not so. In fact, many people who mention suicide are actually crying out for help and must be taken seriously. If they do not receive the attention they need, many will attempt suicide. Sometimes a serious suicide attempt is preceded by a radical change in the person's style of dress or hair, apparently in a desperate attempt to alter his or her situation. It is also common for a person who has decided on suicide to spend a few days "clearing up business" by returning borrowed items, for example, giving away valued possessions, and saying good-bye to friends. Often a person who is prepared to commit suicide appears calmer and less depressed than before. Unfortunately, this often leads many people to believe that the threat has passed.

Thoughts of suicide are common responses to moderate depression or to a stressful event in one's life, but should still be taken seriously. If a person begins speaking of suicide or admits being preoccupied with thoughts of his or her own death, that person should get help immediately. Although it may sometimes be difficult for a person to talk to an authority figure about a friend's troubles, the effort may often be worthwhile. Even if the friend learns about it, he or she is apt to be grateful for the person's concern.

ANXIETY DISORDERS AND NEUROSES

It is true that all people are neurotic in some small way; their psychological shortcomings cause them to be less successful or less happy than they would be otherwise. True neurotics, though, are disabled to some degree by their symptoms. Neurotics live in a world of pain in which mental problems seriously interfere with normal everyday functioning.

The imprecise terms *neurosis* and *neurotic* are now seldom used by mental health professionals, yet their common use by the public gives a fairly accurate impression of this group of disorders. In general, the neuroses include symptoms that are expressions of anxiety, depression, or other emotional disturbances.

Anxiety is a common experience. Ordinarily, when a person is in danger, he or she feels fear. When the danger passes, the fear dissipates. Anxiety is a sort of ongoing fear that will not go away. Mild anxiety can be expressed in many different ways. Usually it is felt as an apprehension or worry. Anxiety in anticipation of a threatening event, such as an important exam or the possible divorce of one's parents, is perfectly normal. Still, if this normal anxiety becomes so great that a person's usual pattern of behavior is disrupted, if he or she cannot function adequately at school

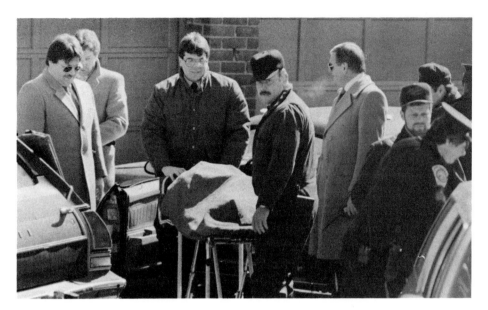

The body of one of four teenagers is removed from the car where the four committed suicide. Statistics show that between 15% and 20% of depressed people eventually commit suicide.

or work, for example, then short-term therapy or counseling may be wise.

Often, however, a person cannot identify the actual threat that is causing the anxiety. In this case, the symptoms of tension, nervousness, and uneasiness simply exist without being directed toward any particular event. The anxiety can also be focused on many trivial things, such as overconcern with being late to a social event, worry about the impression one is making on others, and so forth.

The anxiety disorders and neuroses described below have traditionally been regarded as the outward expression of hidden anxieties. In most cases, the sufferer experiences the anxiety but misunderstands, or fails to identify, the cause.

In a panic disorder, a person feels a sudden overwhelming fear for no apparent reason. The panic usually subsides after a few minutes, but it leaves the victim shaken and fearful of a recurrence. Many victims develop a fear of leaving home, called agoraphobia, because unfamiliar places seem to trigger the attacks.

Separation anxiety occurs in children and teenagers. In this case, an anxiety attack occurs whenever one is separated from family members to whom one is attached. Going to school, for example, causes great distress.

Phobias are irrational fears of common objects or situations. Many phobias develop from a rational fear, as when a child who has been bitten by a dog becomes afraid of all dogs. However, the phobia is often nonsensical, as in a fear of birds or the number 13. A phobia is regarded as neurotic when it disrupts a person's life; often the victim is embarrassed by the irrational fear and tries to hide it from others. Some psychologists, called behaviorists, reject the idea that phobias (and many other disorders) are symptoms of anxiety. They believe that phobias have simply been learned through association with painful events. Behavioral therapy, essentially reeducating the phobic person not to fear the object, has been a very successful treatment.

Sometimes an anxious person is not directly aware of the anxiety. An obsessive-compulsive disorder, for example, seems to be a way of expressing anxiety through pointless rituals. An obsession is a thought or idea that keeps running through one's mind. A compulsion is a repetitive, irrational behavior, such as counting all the ceiling tiles in a room. This sort of behavior is common in normal individuals, especially children. Standardized rituals are also often seen in people who must perform a difficult physical task, as when a baseball pitcher always touches his cap and shoulder before his windup. But a true compulsive struggles to resist the impulse and feels as though he or she is driven to perform the behaviors. They may be continued even when they are clearly damaging, as when a woman washes her hands until they are raw and bleeding. The obsessive-compulsive individual is often very neat and orderly and spends a great deal of time cleaning and arranging possessions.

There are a number of theories of how obsessions or compulsions are related to anxiety. One suggests that compulsions begin as rational childhood behaviors and then come to be applied in inappropriate situations. For example, parents who insist that a child always be scrupulously clean create in the child anxiety about dirt and germs that is relieved by frequent hand washing. Later, anxiety from completely unrelated sources, such as fear of school, is relieved in the way the child has learned best: by washing his hands. Of course, the relief is only temporary; it does not eliminate the true source of the worry, so it must be repeated over and over. According to another theory, obsessions may later replace the compulsions because they are secret (since they are carried out in the person's head) and so are less embarrassing to the sufferer. For example, an obsession with counting the number of words on a page, or with thinking a certain sentence over and over can be less disruptive publicly, and certainly less noticeable than a compulsion to touch each piece of furniture upon entering a room.

Hypochondria is a sort of obsession with the body's health. A hypochondriac is convinced that every little twinge or ache is a symptom of a major illness. The hypochondriac may spend a great deal of time and money seeing doctor after doctor, and may be seriously endangered by multiple exploratory operations and prescribed drugs. Hypochondria is very difficult to treat. In fact, psychiatrists William Good and Jefferson Nelson recommend that physicians not even try to treat it, but rather simply support the patient with constant attention and harmless physical treatments.

The hysterical neuroses include some of the most striking and fascinating psychiatric disorders. They have in common a conversion of anxiety into physical disability or a disruption of normal personality or consciousness. Most of the disorders are more common among women than men. In one type of hysteria, called a conversion reaction, the victim suddenly loses the use of an organ or body part, or loses sensation in it. A pianist may lose feeling in his or her fingertips, for example, or a student may wake up deaf one morning.

At first, it appears that some neurological damage has occurred, but the loss of function does not accord with what is known about physical disabilities. A "blind" person may blink when a light is flashed in his or her eyes, for example. In ancient times, reports of people being "struck blind" or "falling lame" were common. In these more sophisticated times, when most people know that this is impossible, the disorder is less prevalent. Interestingly, it has been proposed that modern faith healers tend to attract those whom medical science has failed to help, namely those with hysterical symptoms. In this sense, then, faith healing can indeed work, at least temporarily. However, the healing occurs in the mind, not in the body, as is often believed.

Hysterical dissociative disorders are disturbances not of physical functions, but of consciousness or personality organization. Amnesia, or loss of memory, may occur in the aftermath of a terrible shock, such as seeing a loved one murdered. Unlike amnesia caused by physical traumas, such as severe automobile accidents, the loss of memory can be selective. Memory is blanked out only for the shocking event, or sometimes only for one's consciousness of oneself, while leaving everyday knowledge intact. Amnesiacs can still drive and know what fashions are current, but cannot recall their name, where they live, or recognize friends. In a related disorder called a fugue, a person suddenly leaves home, forgets his or her past life, and, in an extreme case, adopts a new identity. Fugues often occur after great stress—death or an earthquake, for example. They are not what is known as amnesia and generally last only several hours to a few days. When the person recovers from the fugue, he does not remember anything that happened during that period. Although there are some cases of people becoming violent during a fugue, for the most part people return to normal with little variance in their lives.

Sleepwalking, or somnambulism, is a very common minor disturbance of consciousness that occurs primarily in children. When this occurs, a person gets out of bed while still asleep, and wanders about. It is difficult to awaken a sleepwalker, and he or she is usually unresponsive to questions or suggestions. Sleepwalking can be dangerous, since the person may fall down the stairs or step out of a window, but it is not usually a symptom of a serious disorder. The majority of sleepwalkers are children who are fatigued or under a great deal of stress. There are usually no lasting effects of the disorder.

Finally, in a multiple personality disorder, two or more distinct personalities exist within the same individual and alternate in taking control of the person's behavior. Some of the personalities are aware of the others, whereas some experience amnesia during the time the person is controlled by another personality. Multiple personality disorders generally appear first in childhood, but may go unnoticed until later in life. Often, the alternate personality will have characteristics that are the opposite of the original personality. A quiet person, for example, will have a loud, outgoing second personality. In many cases, the other personality will have a proper name or a title as well. The disorder appears to be chronic, although some cases are less severe than others.

Eating Disorders

Being overweight is a common problem for adolescents. Although sometimes associated with anxiety or depression, it cannot be considered a symptom of emotional disturbance by itself. But some teenagers who are obese (weigh greater than 20% more than the recommended weight for their height) do suffer from an eating disorder. Many of these teenagers are compulsive overeaters—people who compulsively eat large amounts of food, regardless of whether or not they are hungry. These people are literally addicted to food, much in the same way a person may be addicted to drugs, alcohol, or gambling. And, as with many other addictions, the addiction to food generally masks an emotional problem that is being avoided. Each time the problem threatens to surface, it is drowned out with food. For example, a young girl afraid of developing close relationships may hide her true feelings under layers of fat. Psychotherapy can help uncover the deeply buried emotional problems, but to reorganize her eating habits, behavior therapy (retraining the girl's eating patterns) is probably most effective.

Anorexia nervosa is a very severe and common eating disorder usually found in adolescent girls and young women. Sufferers of this disorder—who are frequently from middle-class families—often have a severely disturbed sense of their own body size. In addition, they may be starving themselves for attention or trying to stop the progress of sexual maturation. Most anorexics need to have a sense of control, and certain situations, such as puberty, are beyond their control. Because of this, anorexics will control the one thing they can—their own bodies. Although to anyone else it is clear that the sufferer is starving herself, she perceives herself as fat, and refuses to eat. Anorexia is fatal in 5% to 15% of patients and is difficult to treat. Individual and family psychotherapy offer the best hope.

Bulimia involves binge eating, which is the consumption of large, often huge, quantities of food at one time. The victim maintains normal weight by alternating the binges with strict dieting, exercise, frequent use of laxatives, or self-induced vomiting. Bulimia is very common. One survey published in the journal *Psychological Medicine* in 1981 found that 19% of college women suffered from this disorder at some time. Bulimia can be dangerous as well, causing occasional stomach rupture from overeating, and sometimes fatal changes in body chemistry due to excessive vomiting. Treatment with antidepressant drugs, therapy, and/or behavioral retraining is often effective.

PERSONALITY DISORDERS

As the term implies, an individual with a personality disorder has an immature or distorted personality that disrupts the person's functioning in day-to-day life. The disorder either handicaps the sufferer's relationships with others, or brings him or her into conflict with society's rules for appropriate behavior.

In some persons, an ordinary personality trait carried to an extreme can lead to an inability to function normally. One who craves affection but who is extremely sensitive to rejection may go beyond shyness to develop an avoidant personality disorder. With this disorder, a person both strongly desires and strongly fears social involvement.

A person with a dependent personality disorder, on the other hand, has never learned to take responsibility for his or her life. The victim is dominated by another person, usually a parent or spouse, or by an institution such as the army.

Three personality disorders seem to be related to the psychoses. A schizophrenic person is socially isolated, uncaring, and emotionally restricted. On the other hand, a person with a schizotypal personality disorder is socially incompetent and has odd, eccentric mannerisms of speech and appearance. Schizotypal people may have strange beliefs, such as being convinced that they can predict the future. These beliefs, however, are not firmly held or bizarre enough to be considered delusions, and the person is not out of touch with reality. Because of this, a schizotypal personality disorder is a less severe condition than schizophrenia.

Individuals with a paranoid personality disorder are extremely suspicious, sensitive to slights, and unable to trust others. They may be irrationally jealous or misinterpret facts to "prove" that others are envious or trying to harm them, but they do not have true delusions.

These three disorders, especially the last, are extremely hard to treat. In general, persons with these disorders do not see anything wrong with their style of behavior. They have little motivation to cooperate with the therapist, and their prognosis is poor.

Certain personality disorders are characterized by unusual emotional responses. These are the borderline, histrionic, narcissistic, and antisocial disorders. Sufferers of borderline personality disorders are impulsive, unstable, and have an exaggerated fear of abandonment or separation. Histrionics act with extreme exaggeration. They respond to every social situation as if it were a play, and they (most histrionics are female) are the stars. Minor setbacks bring tantrums, and happy or sad events generate exaggerated emotional displays.

Narcissism is named after the Greek myth of Narcissus, a vain and handsome youth who fell in love with his own reflection. Those with a narcissistic disorder are extremely egocentric and have an inflated sense of their own self-worth. They direct conversations to themselves and take advantage of others.

Antisocial persons feel little guilt or regret for their behavior. They tend to be irresponsible, selfish, and manipulative. Formerly known as psychopaths or sociopaths, these people may at first appear charming but are usually incapable of forming warm human relationships. Not surprisingly, they are often in trouble with the law, and may become professional criminals.

Substance Abuse

Alcoholism and drug abuse are very serious social problems, especially among teenagers. These disturbances can seriously disrupt a person's ability to function in day-to-day life. Psychologically, the alcohol or drug abuser has a personality disorder involving a dependence upon chemical substances. As with the other disorders in this category, a susceptibility to chemical dependence seems to result from inadequate personality development.

The causes of substance abuse are complex and controversial. People can abuse a number of substances, including illicit drugs, prescribed drugs, alcohol, or, as in the case of eating disorders, food. Because substance abuse can be so costly, it is imperative to seek treatment. Abusers who are motivated to change can overcome their dependence through a wide variety of treatment programs. It has been estimated, for example, that between 30% and 50% of treated alcoholics improve significantly. Many do so through the help of Alcoholics Anonymous (AA), founded in the 1930s to help alcoholics learn to cope with their problem. AA members refer to themselves as "recovering" alcoholics, believing that alcoholism is a disease they will never be "cured" of—instead, they must reconquer their addiction every day.

MULTIPLE DIAGNOSES AND MIXED DISORDERS

It is common for someone to have more than one disturbance at a time. Sometimes the disturbances appear to be different symptoms of the same underlying disorder, as when a person has both compulsions and separation anxiety. Sometimes one causes another, as when a depressed person becomes dependent on alcohol to raise his or her mood. And some people just seem to have had the bad luck to be afflicted with two or more disorders independently.

In other cases, patients seem to have a single disorder that mixes the symptoms of two or three others. One example of a mixed disorder is acute schizo-affective illness. With this illness, the patient is either depressed or in an excited, manic state, yet also has the disturbed thinking and hallucinations of schizophrenia. Some researchers believe that acute schizo-affective illness is a variation of manic depression in which the emotional disturbance is so acute as to disrupt the thought processes; others suspect it is a distinct disease.

The diagnosis of a mental or emotional disorder is not a simple process. Clinicians make a diagnosis only after carefully observing and listening to the patient, and sometimes after analyzing the results of psychological tests. These two approaches to diagnosis, observing and testing, are described in the next two chapters.

•   •   •   •

CHAPTER 3

· · · · · · · · · · · · ·

DIAGNOSIS: OBSERVING THE PATIENT

Signs of mental illness may be obvious even to the untrained observer, or they may be subtle, nothing more than a few peculiarities of behavior or signs of anxiety. In either case there is no secret formula for diagnosis. The therapist simply observes the patient's behavior closely and knows the right kinds of questions to ask in order to draw forth the patient's unique patterns of thought.

DIAGNOSIS

It is not enough simply to classify a patient as "psychotic," "depressed," "anxious," or the like. The clinician strives to define more precisely the underlying pathology. The task is frequently difficult. For example, a large dose of cocaine or amphetamines can produce symptoms of psychosis identical to those of paranoid schizophrenia.

Often, however, psychiatrists can arrive at a preliminary diagnosis of a patient's mental disorder within an hour of examining him or her. This is achieved through a thorough examination of the patient's thought processes, emotions, and behaviors.

EVALUATING THOUGHT PROCESSES

If the interviewer suspects some disturbance of thinking, he may conduct what is called a "mental status examination." This is a series of problems and tasks designed to evaluate both logical and emotional responses.

One symptom of psychosis is lack of "orientation," which determines whether patients know who and where they are, and what day and year it is. It is common for schizophrenics to be confused as to where they are, but if the patient is instead disoriented as to what day it is, then the psychiatrist should suspect that the problem is depression or a brain dysfunction. The clinician must also be alert for "factual" information that does not make sense from a rational point of view. Is it reasonable to believe, for example, that a little old lady is being spied on by her landlord? If not, paranoia or paranoid schizophrenia may be a possibility. The severity of such delusions can be assessed by their resistance to logic and the degree of conviction with which they are held. If someone can admit that perhaps his or her view of reality might be incorrect, it is less serious than the delusion of someone who can see no flaws in his or her ideas.

Another strong indicator of psychosis is hallucinations—seeing or hearing people or noises that are not there. Interestingly, however, the senses affected by hallucinations are typically different for different disorders. Hallucinations in schizophrenia or manic-depressive illness are almost always auditory—that is, the sufferer is "hearing things," especially voices. Visual hallucinations, on the other hand, are a symptom of brain disorders, and hallucinations involving the sense of touch (feeling bugs crawling under the skin, for example) usually result from cocaine or alcohol abuse.

Lack of attention and concentration may also indicate psychosis. To test this, the examiner might read a short list of numbers and ask the patient to repeat them. Disorders such as mania and depression frequently interfere with concentration. In these cases, the patient may be unable to remember and repeat the numbers. The patient's general activity level can also be revealing. A manic may be restless and high-strung; some depressed persons can be agitated; others, lethargic.

Extremely free flowing, excited speech also suggests psychosis, but the examiner must listen carefully to the ideas being expressed. An inability to control the flow of thinking, or "loose associations," in which one idea triggers off another in an illogical manner, suggests schizophrenia. One schizophrenic revealed this problem when he said, "I lived with my mother all those years. Even though she sewed well I never had a tear in my pants." On the other hand, if the train of thought proves to have logical connections, but is simply moving with dizzying speed, mania is more likely.

Of course, people are more tolerant of unusual behavior and speech in young children because they expect less conformity to society's rules when the rules have not been fully learned. A four-year-old who says illogical things or talks to an imaginary friend is cute. A 20-year-old who does the same is disturbed.

Sometimes a psychotic can compensate for deteriorating thought processes and maintain a seemingly normal front. Gerald Ross Pascal, a distinguished psychologist and author of *The Practical Art of Diagnostic Interviewing*, reports the case of a successful scientist whose only complaint was that she was "losing energy because of the chemicals she worked with." A thorough medical exam showed no sign of a physical problem. Largely on the basis of her absolute refusal to accept the medical evidence (such rigid defenses suggest a hidden psychosis), Pascal concluded that she was psychotic. He was proven tragically correct when the medical team, appealing to the patient's objectivity as a scientist, forced her to accept their findings. Her defenses collapsed in a "decompensation"; she became openly confused in her thinking, and she had to be hospitalized. People with psychoses often compensate for their illness—justifying their sickness in their minds and acting as "normal" as possible. "Decompensation" occurs when a psychotic is unable to mask his or her illness.

Language skills can reveal a wide range of mental disturbances. Simplistic or overly concrete answers may indicate diminished mental capacity. To test abstract thinking skills, the therapist might ask for an interpretation of a proverb, such as "What does it mean to say, 'Too many cooks spoil the broth'?" or a reasoning task such as "How are an apple and banana alike?" Here the examiner must know the patient's background and prior level of intelligence and education in order to judge his or her answer. Language and thinking skills that would be perfectly normal in a mildly retarded person might be a sign of disturbance in a college professor.

Memory may also be tested. An examiner might ask the patient to recall something that occurred two minutes ago, two weeks ago, and five years ago. Memory losses at different periods have

Because children have not learned all of society's "rules," less is expected of them, and strange behavior is not noted with alarm. In an adult, however, such behavior is often an indication of mental illness.

different meanings. A senile person may have an intact memory for childhood events, yet be confused about something that occurred only a few days previously.

Evaluating Emotions

Thoughts, behaviors, and external events all affect emotion, sometimes in ways that are unclear to an outside observer or even to the patient. When a therapist understands how a particular event affects the patient's emotions, he or she has gained an understanding of the client's psychological processes. As Gerald Ross Pascal writes, "The examiner needs to be as familiar with 'psychological anatomy' as does a surgeon with physical anatomy." In the same way that the surgeon must know how body parts connect, the clinician must discover how a particular person's mind is put together.

In his book *Talking with Patients*, psychiatrist Brian Bird tells of a young woman patient who, after only a few visits, told him that she felt he was the best, the most reliable, the kindest doctor in the whole country. Rather than accepting this compliment or brushing it aside in embarrassment, Bird realized that it had a deeper meaning. He asked her if she had something very important to tell him. Surprised, she admitted that this was true. She had decided to reveal that she had once had an abortion— a guilty secret that had been gnawing at her for years. In order to bring herself to confess this even to her psychiatrist, she had had to convince herself that he was the ideal doctor and the most trustworthy.

Sometimes the patient's emotions are "flattened"; that is, the patient shows little response when describing something wonderful or terrible. This is common among psychotics and the seriously depressed. Other patients, especially hysterics, are overemotional, exaggerating their feelings for public display. Inappropriate emotional responses are easy for the therapist to detect. A young man who describes the failures and disappointments of his present life, smiling all the while, even when the therapist points out the seriousness of his situation, is certain to be covering up his true feelings. As most people know, failure causes pain. This pain must be going somewhere—if not into an emotional expression, then where? The therapist must discover what has become of the missing feelings.

EVALUATING BEHAVIOR

Many therapists look for clues to their patients' situations by noting and interpreting certain behaviors. For example, they may analyze body language. Facial expressions, posture, and speech rhythm can all speak eloquently of a patient's distress.

Appearance is also often a telling sign of a patient's emotional state. Each person's style of dressing, for example, says something about him or her. People's clothes usually reflect age, social position, and status. A conservative businessman is expected to wear a dark suit, a teenager wears jeans or the latest fashions, and so on. Extreme deviations from this, such as a 60-year-old woman wearing a leather miniskirt with a tank top, may represent a deliberate statement of personal style, a lack of social skills, or may reflect a confusion of identity. In each case, odd clothing may reveal something about a person. Even an unusually neat and tidy appearance may lead the clinician to look for other evidence of obsessive-compulsive behavior.

Body movement and position also communicate information. Often the body language that a person expresses contradicts his or her verbal message. As Pascal writes, "If a young lady sits before us with her legs twisted like a pretzel and avoids looking at us and then tells us that she had a very happy relationship throughout her life with her father and other important men in her life, we are very skeptical of what she says. The behavior we observe and the reports of her early experiences do not jibe."

The patient's manner of speaking can also be revealing. The majority of patients are probably nervous or anxious, at least during the first interview. They are in an unfamiliar, uncomfortable situation in which their fears are very much on their minds. This is apt to be indicated by halting or speeded-up speech, speaking too loudly or softly or in a monotone. They also may have difficulty addressing certain topics. An astute interviewer gains as much information from what is not said as from what is said.

THE PSYCHOLOGICAL HISTORY

The roots of many forms of mental illness lie in childhood. One child learns to avoid pain by withdrawing and avoiding others. Other children find that throwing a temper tantrum or lashing out violently brings relief from distress. These general patterns of dealing with life's problems become ingrained in the personality as the child matures into an adolescent and then an adult. The patient's descriptions of events in childhood, even seemingly inconsequential ones, can reveal both the pressures with which the child had to contend and the behavior patterns adopted to deal with them.

The therapist will want a complete history of the problem. If symptoms appeared suddenly, they can also be expected to clear up fairly quickly. If they developed gradually, over a period of years, they are likely to be more resistant to treatment.

This history can even extend back to before the patient's life began. The therapist may want to know of any unusual circumstances surrounding the mother's pregnancy and delivery, and perhaps also if there is a history of mental disturbance in the family.

The therapist will also want to know how well the patient is functioning at present. Does he or she do only the minimum to maintain a normal-appearing existence? Or does he or she have hobbies, interest, and friends who provide support when things go wrong?

INTERVIEWING OTHERS

In many cases, the therapist will want to talk to other people who have observed the patient's behavior in a wide variety of situations. These might include parents or other family members, teachers, or the patient's physician. How much emphasis is put on interviewing others depends on the nature of the patient's problem. If, for example, the difficulty seems to center on family relationships, the therapist should see the family together to gain insight on how they interact.

If the patient is a child or adolescent, the therapist usually interviews the parents. Of course, the therapist does not necessarily accept their reports as perfectly accurate. He or she knows that people who are themselves involved in the disturbed situation have their own motives and biases. Often a therapist will ask for such an interview with two purposes in mind: to gain objective information and to observe the mental state of the parents themselves. Personality patterns, including those leading to neurotic behavior, evolve out of interpersonal relationships.

Sometimes these relationships are distorted and unhealthy. Common symptoms and causes of unhappy family relationships include the domination of one family member over another, alcoholism, and "enmeshment," when family members (usually a parent) are so deeply involved in one another's lives that they do not allow their children to develop their own individual identities. When relationships have been distorted, whether by others, such as disturbed parents, or by the patient's own deteriorating emotional state, stresses develop in the family. These tensions can feed back to the patient, worsening his or her condition.

THE MEDICAL HISTORY AND PHYSICAL EXAMINATION

A thorough mental examination should also include a medical history and physical exam. The date of the first occurrence of symptoms is important in the diagnosis of many mental illnesses. For example, according to the DSM-IIIR, schizophrenia almost always begins before the age of 45, whereas manic-depression can develop later.

In addition, hundreds of physical conditions can directly or indirectly affect one's mental state. For example, some children or elderly people have hearing problems that may make them appear to be withdrawn and uncommunicative, and in turn cut them off from interacting with others. A serious illness in childhood may affect personality development, or may have an indirect effect when parents remain overprotective even after their child has fully recovered. Sometimes the patient's disturbance is not psychological but organic; that is, caused by physical damage to or disease in the brain. Organic brain syndromes, which result from a malfunctioning of large areas of the brain, are often mistaken for psychoses.

There are many causes of organic brain syndrome. These include a deficiency of the hormone produced by the thyroid gland (thyroxine), severe hypoglycemia (low blood sugar), liver or kidney failure, and infections of the brain. Organic brain syndrome can also result from overdoses of many types of drugs, including cocaine, hallucinogens, or certain types of prescription drugs, including antidepressants. All of these occurrences can cause symptoms such as memory impairment, disorientation (especially loss of a sense of the passage of time), confusion, anxiety, and visual hallucinations. These symptoms can, in turn, be mistaken for signs of mental illness.

There are a number of other diseases that can cause symptoms resembling those of mental illness. Huntington's chorea, a hereditary disease of the brain that affects middle-aged people, can be confused with schizophrenia. Some forms of epilepsy—a brain disorder characterized by seizures of varying degrees of severity—can also be mistaken for schizophrenia, or occasionally for mania. Symptoms of Addison's disease, a disorder in which the adrenal glands (the endocrine glands located on top of the kidneys) decrease their production of steroid hormones, can be mistaken for depression or anorexia nervosa. Manifestations of cancer of the pancreas or a malfunctioning thyroid gland can also mimic those of depression, and a very few patients mistakenly diagnosed as neurotic actually have Wilson's disease, a disorder passed on genetically and marked by liver complications and an inability to metabolize copper.

Several drugs or other chemicals can also lead to mental disturbances. For example, medications for high blood pressure can cause depression, steroid hormones can cause symptoms similar to those of manic-depression, and the lead poisoning that children get from eating flakes of old lead-based paint may cause intellectual impairment and hyperactivity.

GETTING AT THE SOURCE OF THE DISTURBANCE

A "textbook diagnosis" is only part of the therapist's exploration of the patient's disturbance. The only way the therapist can fully understand a mental or emotional disturbance is by truly getting to know the patient. The therapist listens not only to what the patient says about himself or herself, but gains an insight into that person by observing his or her unique ways of thinking and reacting.

EXPLORING THE PROBLEM

Robert Kruger and Julian Lieb, authors of a chapter on interviewing for the book *Clinical Psychiatric Medicine*, wrote that "clinical interviewing is the work of a skilled craftsman." Like a craftsman, a therapist is both a scientist and an artist. The interviewer must have a disciplined, scientific knowledge of both normal and abnormal psychology, combined with the creativity to see the world from a completely unfamiliar perspective: that of the mentally ill person. But how does the therapist go about getting to know the patient?

Once they have settled into their chairs in the initial interview, the therapist's first question for the patient is likely to be something to the effect of "What seems to be the trouble?" The therapist is asking for the "presenting problem"—the complaint that brought the patient in for treatment. If the patient answers directly, for example, "My boyfriend and I broke up a month ago, and I've been depressed ever since," the obvious response would be to explore this answer further. How long did the relationship last? What did the patient expect from it? Did this sort of thing happen before? How did her depression affect her, specifically? A sympathetic and sensitive therapist need not ask too many questions directly. Once a conversation gets going, he or she can subtly direct it toward the topics that need to be clarified.

Sometimes the patient cannot really pinpoint what is wrong. With an answer such as "I don't really know what the problem is—I just feel unhappy," the interviewer's job is more difficult. In these cases, the therapist must design questions and comments to encourage the patient to be more specific, both about his or her feelings and the causes of those feelings. Kruger and Lieb noted that the therapist's job then becomes similar to a journalist's. Both are presented with a confusion of reports that have to be structured into a coherent story, with choices made as to what is important and must be investigated further, and what is irrelevant and may be safely ignored.

Besides uncovering the facts, or at least the patient's perception of the facts, the interviewer must also bring out the patient's habits of thinking and behaving. In the same way that every person has a distinctive style of writing and speaking, each person has a style of reacting to stress, whether the tension comes from the outside or is the creation of that person's mind. When frustrated, one person might become angry, another depressed; a third might pretend that nothing is wrong. Each person carries

Although many people enjoy close personal relationships, those with mental disturbances often cannot sustain a healthy interpersonal bond.

these habitual styles of thinking into all areas of his or her life, and they form a major part of that person's personality.

A good interviewer tries to get the patient to describe both general impressions and specific events. Often the two do not match up, and the discrepancies are revealing. Author Gerald Ross Pascal described in his book separate interviews conducted by himself and an inexperienced student on the same patient. The student's summary was bland and conventional. On the patient's relationship with his father, the student obtained reports that the father was a good man and took his son to football games, on fishing trips, and shared other activities with him.

Pascal's interview, however, went deeper. At every vague, predictable statement, he probed for details. Did the patient remember a single actual football game he attended with his father? He did not. How many fishing trips had his father taken him on? The patient could recall only one. And what did he remember of that trip? The patient's most vivid memory was of being yelled at by his father for not knowing how to bait a hook. So the patient, in his interview with the student, was trying to maintain his own image of an ordinary, happy childhood. Pascal's probing revealed that this was an illusion—that the father had actually been cold and uncaring.

Teenagers have especially complex thoughts and emotions. The emotional variability of adolescence often leads to a sense of powerlessness—hence, vulnerability. In his book *Getting to Know the Troubled Child*, psychiatrist David Looff wrote, "The adolescent is always struggling, either successfully or unsuccessfully, with a range of developmental tasks" that require a great effort to master. These tasks include breaking away from the family's restrictions, establishing a firm sense of identity, understanding the power he or she has to influence people and events, establishing successful relationships with peers and with the opposite sex, and mastering the demands of new activities such as sports, part-time jobs, and driving. "All these tasks," Looff pointed out, "with their attendant feelings, daily weigh upon the adolescent."

THE DIAGNOSIS, TREATMENT PLAN, AND PROGNOSIS

Observations of the patient's thought processes, emotional reactions, and behavior, supplemented with information from a medical exam and psychological testing (described in the next chapter), may all be used to produce a formal diagnosis. After deciding what the problem is, the next step is the formulation of a treatment plan.

Tied together with the plan is the therapist's prediction of how the patient can be expected to respond to the treatment. This is known as the prognosis. Certain illnesses may improve with only minimal therapy, whereas others, including most forms of psychoses, do not offer much hope of improvement. Also, as mentioned above, the earlier in a person's life the symptoms appear, the more difficult they are to treat. Someone who has avoided dealing with people since childhood has simply never learned the social skills necessary to function around others. In such a case, it may be difficult or impossible to turn back the clock on the patient's personality development.

•   •   •   •

CHAPTER 4

DIAGNOSIS: TESTING FOR DISTURBANCE

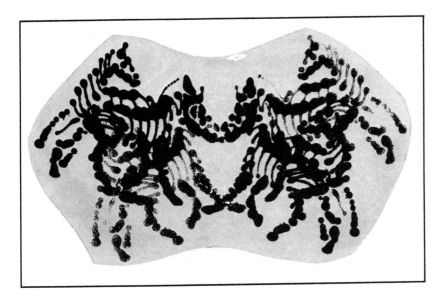

A Rorschach inkblot test.

When it was time for a Cheyenne Indian boy to join the men in a war party, he was expected to engage in a solemn ceremony. Two deep cuts were made in the skin of the boy's chest, and a length of cord was passed through them and tied to the top of a tall pole. As the ceremony continued, the boy had to lean back and tear the cord out through his skin.

A sailor in the U.S. Navy wants to serve aboard a submarine. Submariners, however, must spend months at a time crowded together, without ever seeing sunlight or breathing fresh air. Not everyone can function well under these conditions, so the sailor must pass a series of psychiatric interviews to show that he can cope under such circumstances.

In July 1988, a woman, unable to have children of her own, kidnapped a newborn baby from a hospital in West Virginia. Two days later, she turned herself in and was ordered to a psychiatric hospital for evaluations.

All of these very different events include a test: the observation of a person's behavior under special, standardized conditions. Testing in one form or another reaches back into prehistory. Stories of testing are common even in the Bible, beginning with Adam and Eve's failure to resist temptation. And in China over 2,000 years ago, written examinations were already required of those wishing to obtain a civil service job.

The 19th-century movement toward humane treatment of the retarded and insane stimulated interest in using tests for diagnosis. As early as 1838, tests to identify different degrees of retardation were published in France. In the 1890s Emil Kraepelin, the German psychiatrist who pioneered the diagnosis of schizophrenia, developed the free-association test. During this examination, the tester reads a series of selected words to which the subject responds with the first word that comes to his or her mind. The tester may say "hot," to which a standard response

Sailors who wish to serve on submarines must undergo psychological interviews to determine if they are fit to endure the conditions therein: tight living quarters and no sunlight for months at a time.

might be "cold." Bizarre or unusual responses are found in many forms of mental disturbances.

Until World War I, all psychological tests had to be given individually by a trained professional—an expensive and time-consuming procedure. During the war, however, a committee of the American Psychological Association developed the first paper-and-pencil tests for intelligence and mental disturbance. These tests could be given to dozens of army recruits simultaneously by a single clerk, allowing the army to weed out those with mental deficiencies or severe emotional disturbances. By 1930, objective tests for college admissions, career guidance, and the diagnosis of mental disorders were already in wide use. Since then, tests have become important in all areas of life, and an enormous amount of research has been conducted on such tests. The *Mental Measurements* series of books, edited by Oscar Buros of the Buros Institute of Mental Measurements, which presents only brief summaries of what others have written about tests, runs to 2,965 pages.

But what do these tests actually measure? In most cases the tests quantify human traits, the special characteristics that make one person different from another. Everyone knows people who exhibit different personality types. Each person knows some people, for example, who are highly intelligent and some who are not, some people who are aggressive, whereas others are shy, and some who are emotionally stable, whereas others are moody. Each person could probably evaluate these traits in each of his or her friends and guess how intelligent, extroverted, depressed, or anxious each one is. Tests, however, can do this same job objectively, cheaply, and, if they are well designed, with high reliability and validity.

RELIABILITY AND VALIDITY

A test is reliable when it is repeatable, consistent, and dependable. A reliable test is like a reliable witness in court. A reliable witness is a person who gives the same testimony on Friday that he or she gave on Monday, and tells essentially the same story in December as in June. The witness's report should also be the same under different circumstances: when interviewed by the police at the scene of the crime, or when cross-examined by the defense lawyer. If his or her story changed over time or shifted depending on whom he or she talked to, this witness could not be trusted.

In the same way, a reliable test gives essentially the same results when it is given at different times and in different situations, assuming the trait that is being measured has not changed. It should also be logically consistent within itself, in that answers to its individual questions should all lead to the same conclusion.

A test is valid when it actually measures what is supposed to be measured. The validity of a test is like the truth of the witness's story. A test "tells the truth" when the results provide professionals with accurate information about the characteristic the test is supposed to measure. If, for example, a test of occupational interest gave different results when given by a person's supervisor than the same test given by a sympathetic counselor, one would say that the test was not reliable.

TESTS IN COMMON USE

A clinician can get to know a person only through understanding his or her personality. For this reason, a patient is often given a "battery" of tests—several different types designed to assess different aspects of his or her mental functioning. These tests might include an intelligence test, an objective personality measure, and one or more projective test.

Intelligence Tests

Most high school students have already taken an IQ test such as the School and College Ability Test (SCAT). Most have also taken the Scholastic Aptitude Test (SAT), which examines only those aspects of intelligence relevant to college performance. Both of these are paper-and-pencil group tests. If, however, a person were seeing a counselor or therapist, he or she would probably be given an individually administered intelligence test in which the examiner sits opposite the person being tested and personally presents him or her with a number of different tasks.

This type of IQ test has several advantages. First, like the group tests, it measures general intelligence, so that the clinician can tell whether the client's school or career achievements are ap-

Mad Woman, *by the 19th-century French painter Théodore Géricault. Because mental illness can take so many forms, accurate and reliable diagnostic tests are necessary.*

propriate for his or her abilities. Second, it allows the examiner to get to know the person being tested, to observe his or her reactions to the difficult intellectual problems presented. Third, it provides separate scales on several different aspects of intellectual functioning. If one scale is much lower than the others, it may suggest brain damage, a learning disability, or a specific intellectual shortcoming.

Self-report Inventories

Many types of mental or emotional disorders can be seen as exaggerations or distortions of normal personality traits. These traits show themselves in people's responses to a wide variety of questions. For example, if two people were asked, "What are you most afraid of?", and one answered, "Failing my math exam," and the other replied, "Losing my friends," their responses would suggest somewhat different personalities. This sort of approach is taken by the Minnesota Multiphasic Personality Inventory, known to everyone in the mental health field as the MMPI.

The MMPI consists of 550 statements to which the person tested responds (usually on a machine-scorable answer sheet) in the categories of "true," "false," or "cannot say." Some of the statements include: "I believe I am being plotted against," "Most people will use somewhat unfair means to gain profit or an advantage rather than to lose it," or "I am worried about sex matters." The answer to any given item tells almost nothing about a person, but when dozens of them are added together, a picture of the person's personality begins to emerge. Answers to many statements related to a particular trait are combined to give 10 separate scores on "clinical scales," originally labeled "Paranoia," "Depression," etc. However, research later showed that scores on the scales did not relate so simply to categories of mental illness (paranoids did not always score highly on the paranoia scale, for example), so consequently these labels have been dropped.

A patient's score for each trait is reported in comparison to others of the same sex and age range. If the patient scores abnormally high on the Depression and Social Introversion scales, for example, the therapist will make a note to ask about these areas during an interview. For diagnosis, the overall pattern of scores on the 10 scales is compared to the patterns typically found in schizophrenics, obsessive-compulsives, and others. These days the pattern comparisons are often done by computer.

One other interesting feature of the MMPI is the availability of three additional scales to indicate lying or faking on the test. People may try to fake their test answers to appear to be more normal than they really are or, in some cases, to appear less so. For example, one testee might try to appear more normal than he or she really is in order to avoid hospitalization, whereas a criminal might attempt to present him- or herself as insane to escape punishment.

Because the MMPI is easy to give and score, and because it was the first widely used objective test of psychopathology (it was developed in the 1930s), an enormous amount of research has been done with the test. Every possible type of personality structure, normal and abnormal, has been studied using the MMPI. Although researchers have developed other objective tests that may be somewhat more valid, the MMPI remains the most popular because the scales it uses to measure personality are so familiar to mental health workers.

Projective Tests

Some psychological tests are objective, like a multiple-choice exam. Others, called projective tests, resemble essay exams in which the answers must be evaluated subjectively. Patients who take projective tests are shown some sort of picture or shape and asked to interpret it. Each person does so in a unique way that reveals his or her personality traits, disturbances of thinking, needs, hopes, and fears. The traditional explanation for how projective tests work is based on the psychoanalytic theory of projection. According to this theory, people tend to minimize their anxieties and failings. They are able to express them, however, by attributing them to other people. Thus, a person who is cynical and suspicious may deny that he or she is so but may be convinced that everybody else is.

Unfortunately for psychoanalytic theory, projection does not seem to be a common occurrence, and does not explain why projective tests work. The modern explanation is that each person has a unique style of thinking that is expressed both in their personalities and in the way they interpret the events around them. The old story of a stranger passing through a small town illustrates this point. After he has gone, the townspeople compare their impressions of him. It turns out that the shoemaker judged him by his boots, the tailor by his coat, the doctor by his cough, and so on. In the same way, all people have traits or habits of thinking that are important to them, and by which they interpret people and situations around them. Someone with a strong need to control events, for example, will tend to evaluate situations in terms of that need: whether they are under control, could be controlled, and so on.

Probably the most familiar example of a projective technique is the inkblot test. Developed by the Swiss psychiatrist Hermann Rorschach in the 1920s, the test consists of a number of abstract inkblots. Usually, 10 different blots are used, 5 in shades of black and gray and 5 with color. The blots are shown to the patient, who describes what he or she sees in them. For example, one patient might describe a blot as "a boy with the head of a lizard, pounding a birthday cake with a shoe. On the side is the face of a dwarf and a sun setting over the palm trees."

Later the examiner computes the number of responses that

fall into various categories, such as human figures, animals, maps, blood, movement, and whether the whole blot or an obscure part of it is used. Certain categories are believed to be related to certain traits; for example, whole-blot responses correspond to conceptual thinking, color responses to emotional thoughts, and human movement to imagination. The examiner may draw specific conclusions about the patient's mental state from these scores, but most researchers believe that the Rorschach test is not valid enough for this. On the other hand, it appears that certain general traits such as hostility and anxiety can be measured reasonably well with the inkblot technique.

Most therapists probably do not use the test scores directly for diagnosis. Rather, the inkblot test provides a standardized, structured way for the therapist to interact with the patient, to observe his or her thought processes at work. In this sense, it is an extension of the diagnostic interview.

The other projective test that is commonly used is the Thematic Apperception Test (TAT). Patients taking the TAT are shown several pictures of people in rather ambiguous situations, and are asked to make up a story about each one. There are a number of methods for scoring the responses, but the most popular is one the test's originator, Henry Murray, a psychiatrist at Harvard University, developed in 1938. Murray's scoring system emphasizes the "needs" expressed in the stories. Some of these include the need for autonomy (independence), affiliation (social relationships), and dominance (the desire to control others).

The system also provides scores for "press," the environmental forces that help or hinder the satisfaction of needs. Examples of press include being attacked by another person, being comforted, or being exposed to physical danger. By combining the scores for needs and press, the clinician can build up a description of both the client's personality and how he or she perceives the world. Like the Rorschach, the TAT is often used simply as a forum for getting to know the client rather than as a formal test.

Many scientists have criticized the TAT as unreliable and invalid. Those professionals who use the TAT, however, believe that despite its limitations, it provides a more accurate understanding of the fundamental nature of the person than objective tests.

CHAPTER 5

GETTING HELP: PSYCHOTHERAPY

Television dramas and movies often make it seem as though caring, love, and sympathy are enough to lead a mentally ill person back to normalcy. Unfortunately, this is not always the case. Naturally, love can help in some ways—for example, it can relieve some of the pain of severe mental disturbances and everyday emotional upheavals—but it is not enough. In the same way that people seek a physician's help if they are in physical pain, it makes sense to get help with emotional pain or disturbed thinking.

TREATMENT PROVIDERS

There are several different types of health-care providers for mentally ill patients. These are psychiatrists, psychologists, other mental health professionals such as social workers, and general health professionals. Each provides a different type of treatment, and each requires special training.

Psychiatrists and Psychologists

The average person probably knows that a doctor of mental illness is a psychiatrist or psychologist but may not understand the difference between the two professions. Psychiatrists are medical doctors who specialize in treating behavior problems for which medicine cannot identify a purely physical cause. They differ from neurologists, who treat disturbances that are known to result from physical injuries or diseases of the brain and nervous system.

The road to becoming a psychiatrist is long, difficult, and expensive. Having first completed a four-year undergraduate program, and after three years of medical school, psychiatric training requires approximately four years of internship and residency, during which the young physician treats patients under the guidance of an experienced psychiatrist.

Clinical psychologists do not attend medical school, but begin their psychological training immediately upon entering graduate school. In some states it is possible to practice in a limited way (as a school psychologist, for example) with only a master's degree. However, most psychologists go on to earn a Ph.D., which requires approximately three years of course work, two years of internship, and a year or two of scientific research in some aspect of psychology.

Nearly half of all psychologists, however, are not trained as therapists, but instead study normal human and animal behaviors in all their tremendous variety. Psychologists might do research on such diverse topics as the workings of the brain, a chess master's decision-making process, racial prejudice, falling in love, leadership, body language, and almost anything else that might be related to how people think and act.

There is a great deal of overlap in the therapeutic techniques of psychiatrists and clinical psychologists. Most, for example, try to find the cause of a patient's problems, suggest some beneficial changes in behavior, and observe the patient's reaction to the suggestion. There are, of course, some differences: Psychologists are more likely to use tests in diagnosis, whereas psychiatrists are more likely to look for physical causes of disturbance. And psychiatrists are qualified to prescribe drugs, something that no other mental health professional can do.

Both psychiatrists and clinical psychologists sometimes specialize, primarily treating children, adolescents, drug abusers, or those with sexual dysfunctions, for example. Some psychiatrists, and a very few psychologists or other mental health professionals, become psychoanalysts. This requires still more intensive training, usually for about seven years. The training involves the study of analytical theories, first developed by Freud and practiced under the direction of a training analyst. Psychiatrists who hope to specialize in psychoanalysis must also undergo analysis themselves to gain insight into their own thought processes.

Other Mental Health Professionals

There are often more psychiatric social workers in a mental health facility than psychologists and psychiatrists combined. Psychiatric social workers are those who have earned a master's degree in social work after two years of graduate study, and who have specialized in psychiatry. Although many psychiatric social workers conduct therapy, they typically believe that the client's problems result from a mismatch between the demands of the situation and the abilities of the person. If a man has difficulty in dealing with people at his job, for example, a psychiatric social worker might help him find another job better suited to his abilities.

Counselors usually receive their graduate instruction in schools of education, which also train teachers and school administrators. There are many different specialties adopted by those with master's degrees in this field. They include guidance counseling, marriage counseling, and family counseling.

A psychiatric nurse may often practice as a therapist or counselor. Becoming a nurse requires two to four years of nursing school, which usually takes the place of college. BSNs (Bachelor of Science in Nursing), however, are nurses who have attended four years of college and have received their bachelor of science degrees in nursing. A fully qualified psychiatric nurse must have a master's degree in nursing.

Other Helping Professionals

Many other health-care professionals have received some instruction in psychotherapy or counseling. Physicians, for example, take courses in psychiatry during medical school, and most

Members of the clergy are trained to listen and offer advice. Many may also be able to recommend a competent therapist or helpful organization.

priests, rabbis, and ministers receive training in counseling at graduate schools that train religious leaders of that particular faith.

These professionals can help a person decide whether or not to seek formal counseling or therapy. If the person in question decides to seek counseling, they can often recommend someone with whom he or she would feel comfortable.

Helping Organizations and Informal Help

One does not have to be a professional to offer help to a troubled person. Most people are probably familiar with such self-help organizations as Alcoholics Anonymous or local suicide-prevention hot lines. In groups such as these, interested laypeople deal constructively with the problems of their peers. They offer support, limited counseling, and a referral service for therapy.

Although not every person feels the urge to join self-help groups, everyone does feel the need at some point in his or her life to share his or her troubles with someone. A person he or she can trust, such as a teacher, coach, relative, or friend, may give that person enough support and informal counseling to make a big difference.

Good intentions, however, do not always guarantee good advice. If the troubled person is more upset or confused after talking to someone than before, the person chosen is probably not a good bet as an informal counselor. A potential adviser should be willing to listen to all the person has to say, and should not minimize the person's problems, or offer superficial advice such as "Just try to look on the bright side."

Philosophies of Treatment

Most psychiatrists and some other therapists adopt what is called the "medical model." This philosophy regards the mentally disturbed person as a patient who needs to be treated for an illness. This point of view was developed in the latter half of the 20th century to make it clear that the sick person is not morally or intellectually inferior and has no reason to feel guilty. The medical model has done much to remove the stigma from disturbed behavior and to encourage troubled people to seek treatment.

Many therapists believe, however, that the medical model has a negative side. They reject the concept of mental "illness," because they believe it encourages passiveness on the part of the victim. For instance, a person who is physically ill can usually just take some medicine and follow the directions of a physician to get better. A person with a mental disorder, however, must work at getting well and must carry some of the responsibility for success or failure. For this reason, many psychotherapists refer to those they treat as "clients" rather than patients. They emphasize that therapy is not something done "to" or "for" a person, but is done "with" him or her.

Also, most mental health providers use some combination of counseling and therapy. In counseling, the provider gives direct advice about what the client should do. In therapy, the assumption is that there is some form of mental or emotional disturbance, and the goal is to make fundamental changes in the person.

THE THERAPEUTIC EXPERIENCE

There are probably as many different types of therapeutic experiences as there are combinations of therapists and clients. No two therapists run their treatment sessions exactly alike, and what they do in the sessions will depend largely on the client and his or her specific problem. Nevertheless, the particular training or theoretical orientation of the therapist has a great influence on what happens in therapy. A behaviorist is interested in identifying the environmental influences that cause the patient to react as he or she does. The rational-emotive therapist wants to identify the illogical ideas that are the cause of the patient's distress. And the psychoanalyst will be interested in the patient's childhood experiences.

The next three chapters explore some of the most important approaches to mental illness. These approaches will be presented in their "pure" forms—the way they were taught by the founders of each of the theories. In each case, some examples of therapy sessions are included. However, most therapists have been influenced to a greater or lesser degree by all of these important theories. The majority of therapists do not adhere strictly to any

Those who work at suicide hot lines not only listen to depressed people but offer information about how and where to get further help.

one approach, but rather choose concepts and methods from the theories that they believe will work in individual cases. Thus, it is impossible to describe a "typical" therapy session.

Seeking Help

For most people, the greatest challenge in psychotherapy is the decision to seek help. Many people who come for treatment are fearful that they will be found to be crazy, abnormal, or unhealthy, although it may be reassuring to know that the therapist is never shocked or alarmed by what the patient has to say. It is entirely natural, however, for a person to feel hesitant about speaking of personal matters to a stranger.

In the same way that a person may be asked to undress for a physician, the therapist expects that person to reveal him- or herself psychologically. This is often difficult and requires a certain amount of courage. Fortunately, the process is easy to get used to, and most clients leave the first interview with the feeling that it was not as bad as they expected it to be.

Although it is important for a person to feel comfortable with his or her therapist, he or she may not feel entirely at ease after the first visit. This is quite normal, and the feeling generally disappears after several more sessions. Once the person comes to know and trust the therapist, he or she will begin to relax and feel more comfortable. It is unrealistic for the client to expect to feel perfectly comfortable with the therapist right away, and he or she should attend several sessions before deciding to change practitioners. If, however, the feeling of discomfort persists, or the patient begins to actively dislike the therapist, he or she should certainly find a new one. The therapeutic relationship is, most naturally, an intimate one, and the patient need not feel guilty for deciding to find a therapist with whom he or she can be more open.

Diagnostic Tests

Whether or not a therapist tests a patient depends on the therapist's background and personal preference, on the presenting problem, and on the setting in which the person is being treated. Some therapists may prefer the objectivity of test scores, whereas others feel that dry facts and figures are not as useful as their own impressions.

The setting in which treatment takes place can also make a difference. Testing is very common whenever some sort of institution or organization is involved, or when objective records of behavior need to be kept. Testing therefore often occurs in schools, prisons, or military service.

Questions

There are a number of questions a patient may want to ask the therapist before he or she begins counseling or treatment. For example, the patient may want to know about confidentiality— that is, whether his or her case will be discussed with anyone else. A therapist will often discuss the problems of a patient who is under 18 with the patient's parents or school officials. If this bothers the patient, he or she should certainly discuss the possibility with the therapist. Another question patients commonly ask is whether they will be hospitalized. A therapist is likely to recommend hospitalization only if a patient seems to be in danger of harming him- or herself or others. Naturally, patients who feel they would benefit from getting out of their current family or school situation should discuss the problem with their therapist.

Most patients also ask about the length of therapy. This is a very difficult question to answer. Certainly the patient should not expect any fundamental changes to occur immediately. It may be a relief to have someone to talk to, but learning new ways to think is usually a slow, difficult process, like learning how to drive. Someone who has not yet learned to drive a car imagines it to be easy—push one pedal to go, another to stop. In fact, it takes intense concentration and a lot of practice. Later, driving becomes second nature and the memory of how difficult it was fades away. In the same way, rational behavior requires careful learning and gets easier with practice.

Group Therapies

Many therapy sessions take place in a one-on-one setting with the therapist and the patient. Often, however, the therapist will see several patients together. This type of treatment—the group therapy session—allows the therapist to help several patients at once and is less expensive to the patient. There is a far more important justification for group therapy than this, however: Humans are social animals. Whether or not they are happy depends a great deal on their relationships with others. If a patient needs to learn new ways of relating to other people, what better way to practice these skills than by trying them out in a group setting? Irwin Yalom, a prominent group therapist at Stanford University, notes in his book *The Theory and Practice of Group Psychotherapy* that "without exception, patients enter group therapy with the history of a highly unsatisfactory experience in their first and most important group—their primary family."

There are probably nearly as many theories of group therapy as there are of individual therapy. One type of group therapy is special, however. In family therapy, the therapist treats the patient and his or her family together. It often makes more sense to see treatment as an attempt to cure a disturbed family than a disturbed individual. Families have personalities distinct from those of their members. Any individual member may be basically healthy, but the group as a whole may have fallen into an unhealthy pattern of interactions. Often one member, usually a child, gets the blame for family disturbances. Over time, this can severely affect the child who plays scapegoat. Family therapy can prove exceptionally valuable in getting to the root of a problem.

• • • •

CHAPTER 6

PSYCHOANALYSIS

Sigmund Freud with his daughter, Anna, and his grandson.

Perhaps no other scientist in the history of medicine contributed so much to the psychiatric specialty and influenced so many practitioners and laypeople as Sigmund Freud. Born in 1856 to Jewish parents and raised in Vienna, Austria, Freud received a medical degree at the age of 25. For several years he conducted biological experiments, but he later received training as a psychiatrist.

Freud was dissatisfied with the explanation of neurosis as the result of physical damage or disease. He struggled to understand the mysterious symptoms that plagued his patients. Why should a woman's arm suddenly become numb? Why should a man be tortured by memories of trivial childhood mistakes? And why did his patients often feel better after talking about past events? Over the course of decades, Freud developed some radical theories about the workings of the unconscious mind and the importance of sexuality. Though they remain controversial, Freud's theories have had a profound effect on the treatment of mental illness.

The Psychoanalytic Theory of Personality and Neuroses

Freud believed that the human personality is composed of three parts: the id, the ego, and the superego. According to psychoanalytic theory, all behavior, especially neurotic behavior, results from the way these three components interact. The *id* (Latin for "it") contains the animalistic forces in human nature. The id is entirely selfish and pleasure seeking, and it demands the immediate gratification of its instinctive urges. These instincts are the sole sources of energy for all of human behavior. Freud's background in biological research convinced him that all animals, including humans, are driven to find nourishment and safety first and then a sexual partner. For most humans, food and safety needs are easily satisfied. Therefore, according to psychoanalytic theory, the sex drive is the most important instinct in humans.

Of course, babies are not born with a sex drive in a way that adults think of the term. The drive, called the libido, may be more accurately thought of as a desire for sensual pleasure. As a child grows up, this desire finds different means of expressing itself until, if all develops naturally, it matures into adult sexuality. Another principal drive of the id is the death instinct, or death wish. Freud developed this idea to explain the violence in human nature, especially war. Human aggression and suicide, Freud concluded, are the outward expressions of an inner wish to die. Why should humans wish to die? Freud knew that all plants and animals grow old and die. He believed that, therefore, humans instinctively know and accept death as inevitable.

A newborn baby's personality consists entirely of id. However, the demands of the id quickly come into conflict with reality,

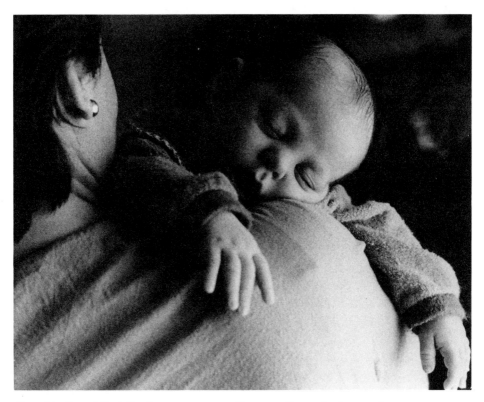

Freud believed that the human personality goes through stages of psychological growth and development, starting in infancy.

which requires sensible, rational behavior. The *ego* (which means "I" in Latin) develops out of the id in order to deal with the realities of the world. Consider this example: If the infant's id screams, "Feed me!" the ego might respond, "You will just have to wait." However, it is not very effective to simply deny the id its desires, so the ego develops ways of partially satisfying the id, often, in effect, by fooling it. When the id demands, "I want my bottle!" the ego responds, "Here, suck on this pacifier instead and you will feel better."

The phrase "he does not know his own mind" suggests that mental processes are occurring that all humans are unaware of. Freud proposed that the id operates entirely on the level of the unconscious, which contains material that cannot be brought into awareness. The ego, however, functions on both the conscious and unconscious levels. The ego is the only part of the mind that can deal consciously with the outside world. All intentional behavior, speech, and thought, therefore, radiate from the ego.

As the child matures, he or she adopts the moral standards and values of adults, especially of parents. These moralistic impulses are contained in the *superego*. The superego is just as irrational and demanding as the id, but its demands are very different. Whereas the id desires instant gratification of needs, the superego demands that the person live a perfect, morally correct life. Needless to say, this leads to a great deal of conflict.

When a woman finds herself struggling to decide whether or not to do something she would like to do, but knows that it is morally wrong, she is dealing with an id/ego/superego conflict. When such a conflict is occurring, a person feels anxious. Since anxiety is painful and unpleasant, the ego protects the person (and itself) by keeping the conflict out of consciousness. It also attempts to satisfy, at least partially, the demands of the id, superego, and the real world. The ego develops "defense mechanisms" to deal with the conflicts that arise from these demands. According to Freud, the central defense mechanisms are repression, regression, displacement, projection, and rationalization.

Repression is the simplest and least effective defense. It consists of merely pushing the conflict out of awareness into the unconscious. This does not resolve the conflict, of course, and the anxiety continues. According to psychoanalytic theory, repression is the source of all neuroses. Sometimes the anxiety is felt directly, which is the anxiety neurosis. In other cases it is bottled up, and the anxious energy is channeled into neurotic symptoms, such as a phobia, a compulsion, or a hysterical paralysis (when a person is unable to move all or part of his or her body without any apparent medical cause).

Regression occurs when the ego fools the person into believing that he or she is less mature and responsible than he or she really is. A person who believes this feels free to act in a way that was formerly unacceptable—for example, throwing temper tantrums or pouting.

Displacement is a defense in which anxiety or hostility is released onto an innocent target. A schoolgirl who is having trouble with classes cannot safely vent her anger at her teacher, so she may come home and scream at her little sister. Many therapists believe that depression occurs when the victim of displacement is oneself. In this way, depression can be seen as anger turned inward.

Projection occurs when a person attributes his or her own unacceptable impulses to another person, then condemns that person for possessing those same character traits. The person then is able to punish or condemn the impulse without threatening his or her own self-image. Rationalization, another defense mechanism, involves admitting one's failures, but proposing seemingly reasonable excuses. A boy who fails to complete school assignments on time (perhaps because of unconscious anger toward his teacher) may explain it to himself as being a result of unrealistic time pressures, the teacher's unclear explanation of the assignment, or another similar excuse. Rationalization is regarded as the most mature of the ego defenses, as it requires consciously acknowledging shortcomings.

STAGES OF DEVELOPMENT

Freud believed that the human personality goes through stages of psychological growth and development that match the stages of physical growth. According to psychoanalytic theory, a person's personality is the result of the way he or she deals with challenges and conflicts at five psychosexual stages. The instinctual energy, especially the libido (which will eventually become the sex drive), is expressed through the particular body part that is important at that stage. In the rare cases of ideal, completely successful development, conflicts or needs that are appropriately resolved or satisfied allow the energy to move on to the next stage. If the person reaches adulthood without conflict, the energy is free to deal with day-to-day problems.

If the child cannot resolve a conflict, or if needs are left unsatisfied or are overindulged at a particular stage, a weakness is left in that aspect of the personality. Part of the energy is continually drained away to deal with the unresolved challenges. This is called a fixation.

To make this concept clearer, imagine a woman who feels she has missed her chance of going to college. This person may spend a considerable amount of time and energy thinking unhappily about the loss of a college education, and daydreaming of what it would have been like—the college years themselves, and all the opportunities that have been lost to her. This time and energy are therefore not available for her everyday tasks.

Overindulgence of needs can also be harmful. For example, if a man attended college and looks back on those years as the best in his life, and every experience after those years has been dull by comparison, this man will also have a problem. He may spend all of his time reliving his old memories—and comparing every event to his college years. In this way he lives excessively in the past and ignores his present needs.

These examples show the under- or oversatisfaction of conscious desires in adulthood. Freudian theory, however, is primarily concerned with unconscious fixations that occur in infancy or childhood because of conflicts that arise during the five psychosexual stages.

During the oral stage (from birth to age one), movements of the mouth are the principal means the baby has of expressing its needs. Besides the desires for nourishment, love, and safety that are satisfied by nursing and crying, the infant has aggressive impulses that are expressed by biting and chewing. If development becomes fixated at this stage, certain oral character traits may be carried into adulthood. These include a continuing desire for using the mouth (such as overeating, smoking, or excessive talking) or oral aggressiveness (making "biting" sarcastic remarks).

During the anal stage (ages one through two), the child experiences pleasure in expelling feces as soon as he or she exerts pressure on the bowels. For the first time, however, the child's needs come into conflict with the wishes of the parents. They demand that the child become toilet trained. One way the child can resist is simply to refuse. This tactic can serve as the model for later ways of dealing with conflict, even in adulthood. This "anal retentive fixation" causes the person to be stubborn and stingy. However, if the parents threaten and bully the child into proper behavior, he or she may become overly fussy, neat, and compulsive about following rules.

The phallic stage lasts until about age five. At first, both boys and girls love the mother and "identify" with her, that is, want to be like her. With the development of the sex organs, the libido begins to take on a truly sexual, though immature, form. The boy begins to feel sexual urges for the closest person of the opposite sex: the mother. The father, however, is a powerful rival for the mother's affections. The child responds with a wish to do away with his father and take his place. Freud named this desire the Oedipus complex, after the mythical Greek king who unknowingly killed his father and married his mother. It is resolved when the boy switches his identification from his mother to his father.

By becoming a miniature version of his father, the son gains in two ways. First, he is protected from the father's anger because he knows the father will not harm someone like himself. Second, by being like the father, he gains the father's privileges, especially the love of the mother. When the boy switches his identification from the mother to the father, he also takes on the man's sexual identity and adult moral values. According to psychoanalytic theory, if this switch does not occur, the son continues to identify with the mother and may grow up to be a homosexual. This theory of homosexuality is highly controversial, however.

A girl in the phallic stage also develops a sexual attraction for the opposite-sex parent, the father. (This is called the Electra complex, after the mythical Greek character who kills her mother

According to legend, the ancient Greek king Oedipus inadvertently married his mother and killed his father. Freud believed that all boys go through an Oedipal stage, when they identify with their mother and envy their father. In most instances this identification is ultimately transferred to the father and the conflict is resolved.

in a Euripides drama.) Her rivalry with the mother is resolved by identifying even more strongly with the same-sex parent. Like the resolution for the boy, this offers her safety and a share in the father's affection. In Freud's time, this meant accepting a passive, dependent role, inferior to that of men.

At the end of the phallic stage, the child enters into a long latency period during which the personality remains relatively stable. At the onset of puberty, with the maturation of the sex organs (around age 12), the genital stage begins. Mature love and sexual expression develop during this period. Although the conflicts that occur during the genital stage may be very stressful and important to the adolescent, they are regarded by psychoanalysts as having less impact on the formation of the personality than the first three stages.

Psychoanalytic Therapy

Freud's theory of personality development and neurosis was based on his experiences with patients who came to him for help. As he constantly revised and deepened his theory, Freud also developed a unique approach to therapy called psychoanalysis. Very complex in nature, psychoanalytic therapy does not often cure the patients' distress as quickly or as effectively as some of the simpler approaches. This will become more evident later in this chapter.

UNCOVERING UNCONSCIOUS CONFLICTS

The basic approach in psychoanalysis is to get the patient to remember and deal with repressed conflicts, including fixations and troubling thoughts and memories. Freud compared these conflicts to ancient ruins hidden under layers of soil (the ego defenses), which preserve them intact. The analyst must excavate until the ruins are revealed to the open air, where natural forces will eventually wear them away. The ultimate goal is to be able to bring to consciousness every troubling event in the patient's life—particularly early childhood. In fact, some people who have been psychoanalyzed claim that they can even remember the trauma of being born.

The analyst helps the patient to unearth these hidden conflicts through conversation in a relaxed setting. One of the most recognizable symbols of psychoanalysis is the couch. The couch is actually used during psychoanalysis; the patient lies on the couch while the analyst sits near the head end, out of the patient's view. Since the patient cannot see the therapist's reactions, he or she is less likely to alter his or her statements in response to the therapist's reactions. What is important, then, is what is in the patient's head and what he or she is discussing, and not the analyst's judgment. For the same reason, the therapist says little during the session except for asking occasional questions meant to direct the patient's flow of ideas. Psychoanalysts do not give advice about problems, but rather try to bring the patients to see for themselves what needs to be done.

DREAMS AND FREE ASSOCIATION

Simply asking the patient to talk about his or her conflicts is usually unproductive, since the important conflicts are unconscious. In order to discover what is going on beneath the patient's awareness, the therapist interprets dreams and free associations. Why do people dream? In Freud's time it was assumed that people dreamed to protect their sleep from disturbing stimuli.

For example, a person may be asleep and hear a phone ring or a doorbell buzz and, instead of waking up, incorporates these disturbing stimuli into his or her dream. In this way, the dreamer gives these disturbances a logical, undisturbing meaning. If a person is dreaming about being in school, for example, he or she might interpret the ringing of the phone as a class bell or the buzzer as the one on the scoreboard in gym. But internal stimuli can be sources of disturbance, too. A sleeping infant may be hungry; its id demands satisfaction. The ego then manufactures a dream about nursing to deceive the id. An adolescent may have sexual desires and dream about sex. Such dreams are called wish-fulfillment dreams.

Disturbing thoughts, fears, and memories can also rise up from the unconscious, threatening a person's tranquillity during sleep. These stimuli, too, are reinterpreted and disguised, allowing the dreamer to deal with the fear-producing ideas without having to face their true meaning.

The analyst listens to the patient's dream and asks probing questions to uncover the connections between people, places, events, and emotions in the dream and those in real life. These connections, or associations, reveal unconscious conflicts. In free association, the patient simply talks. Sometimes the therapist says a few words and asks for reactions to them, but usually the patient just thinks out loud, expressing whatever thoughts pop into his or her head. The topics the patient chooses, or avoids, reveal a great deal to a trained analyst.

ANALYSIS OF RESISTANCE

As the analysis approaches a sensitive topic, the patient may raise his or her ego defenses. He or she may suddenly break off the free association, change the subject, or fail to make an obvious connection. These resistances alert the therapist that the patient is repressing an important conflict. Psychologist Daniel Wiener reports a dialogue (in his 1968 book *A Practical Guide to Psychotherapy*) that took place during the first session between a male patient, J. P., and an analyst.

> Dr. R.: How did you feel about your father?
> J. P.: I hated him when he made me do things. I hated him to be mean to mother. But I felt sorry for him too.
> Dr. R.: And your mother?
> J. P.: She was complaining all the time about him and crying. I felt sorry for her. . . . But why should she always cry to me about him?
> Dr. R.: What did you feel toward your mother for doing this?
> J. P.: I hated it. I hated every minute of it.
> Dr. R.: And her? How did you feel about her?
> J. P.: I hated it. I don't know. It wasn't her fault, I guess. She couldn't help it. She needed someone to talk to.
> Dr. R.: It's hard for you to say how you felt toward her then?
> J. P.: I don't want to say I hated her. But I must have. I guess I did.

In this exchange, the therapist immediately notices that J. P. avoids saying how he felt about his mother, and instead describes her behavior. Over the next series of questions, or prompts, Dr.

R. gently but persistently brings him back toward this topic, confirming the resistance. Eventually the patient admits the painful thought: that he did hate his mother. This is the process that Freud was referring to when he spoke of excavating hidden conflicts. However, if J. P. had continued to avoid the issue or deny it, Dr. R. would not have persisted, since a direct challenge to him would only have caused a strengthening of ego defenses.

CATHARSIS AND INTERPRETATION

After the doctor and patient have uncovered a painful, previously repressed memory, the process of "wearing away" must begin. The analyst encourages the patient to reexperience the traumatic event in full force, which releases the pent-up emotional pressure. With less internal stress to contend with, the ego can lower some of its defenses, thus freeing up energy for productive work. This release of emotions is called catharsis. It may take many repetitions of catharsis for the traumatic memory to begin to lose its emotional power.

Another means of "wearing away" at exposed conflicts is interpretation. In time, the analyst forms a hypothesis, or educated guess, about the causes of a patient's disturbance. If the patient seems ready, the therapist will suggest an interpretation. For example, Dr. R. suggested that J. P. had strong emotional conflicts toward his mother. In this case, J. P. accepted the interpretation, discovered something new about himself, and was consequently able to deal with the conflicts on the conscious level. After dozens of such interpretations, some simple and obvious, some complex and difficult to accept, the patient achieves a profound understanding of his or her problems. With this understanding comes a measure of control, and, finally, relief.

FREUD'S INFLUENCE

The work of Sigmund Freud had and still continues to have an enormous impact on all areas of psychology, psychiatry, and psychotherapy. Many therapists accept to some degree the basic propositions of Freudian theory: that early childhood experiences are important, that unconscious conflicts drain away energy that would otherwise be used in a productive manner, and that defenses are erected to protect the personality from threat. It is widely felt, however, that there are some flaws in Freud's psychoanalytic model.

Psychoanalysis is not the best treatment for all. First, a patient must have a great deal of time and money to invest in analysis. A fundamental principle of the theory is that neuroses and personality disorders are deeply rooted in the unconscious. Therefore, analysts believe that therapy must be a painstaking process of bringing unconscious conflicts to the surface. Many traditional psychoanalysts maintain that patients cannot begin to make progress without at least an hour a day of therapy, 4 days a week, for 3 to 5 years—a total of at least 760 hours in treatment. Group therapy, however, allows the therapist to help more than one patient at a time and, in addition, saves the patient a great deal of money.

Certain mental illnesses are not likely to be helped by psychoanalysis. If the illness seriously disrupts the person's life or causes intense pain, the patient clearly cannot wait for years to get relief. Psychotics also cannot be effectively treated by psychoanalysis because their thought processes are too disorganized to allow them to gain an understanding of the causes of their problems.

In addition to these problems with the effectiveness of psychoanalytic therapy, there have been many challenges to the theory behind psychoanalysis. Of the thousands of attempts to test the basic assumptions and conclusions of the Freudian system, only a few have supported the theory. The overall conclusion is that most of the propositions of psychoanalytic theory cannot be validated by scientific methods. Nonetheless, there are still many analysts committed to Freud's original ideas.

NEO-FREUDIAN THEORIES AND THERAPIES

Although Freud's genius attracted many disciples, several of them broke away to develop their own theories and methods of therapy. These "neo-Freudians" accepted many of the basic principles of psychoanalytic theory, but differed with Freud on others. Carl Jung, Alfred Adler, and Karen Horney were three of the most influential neo-Freudians.

Carl Jung was Freud's greatest disappointment. Freud was concerned that psychoanalysis would always be associated with the narrow world of Viennese Jewish intellectuals, and had hoped that Jung, who was Swiss, a Christian, and a highly regarded psychiatrist in his own right, would inherit the leadership of the movement. But the independent, mystical Jung had other ideas. In particular, he rejected Freud's belief in the importance of childhood sexuality, and put more emphasis on nonsexual, frightening events. He also developed the idea of the collective unconscious, which he believed contained archetypes—ideas or images that had developed over the entire history of the human race. Finally, he refused to accept Freud's pessimistic view of human nature as a struggle against destructive unconscious forces, and believed instead that people are positive, striving, and goal oriented. Jung's therapy was similar to Freud's, with emphasis on dream interpretation and delving into the unconscious, but he believed that conflicts and crises in adulthood were more important than those in childhood.

Alfred Adler also rejected Freud's ideas about sex. Adler, who introduced the term inferiority complex, believed that it was the child's discovery of his inferior status and lack of power that was the ultimate cause of neurosis. Adler was also the first to develop the concept of self-esteem as an important component of personality. His therapy focused on social relationships in the patient's life, helping him or her to develop effective strategies for coping with others.

Karen Horney, an early feminist, disputed Freud's views on women. Freud often saw women as inherently inferior to men, and thus deserving of second-class status. Horney blamed the inequality of women on their powerless position in society. She also emphasized the child's need for feelings of security, free from parental rejection or overprotection. Lack of security, she felt, leads neurotics to develop an idealized, unrealistic image of themselves. In her therapy, Horney attempted to eliminate the irrational solutions that her patients often devised to deal with their human relationship problems.

Swiss psychologist Carl Jung rejected Freud's emphasis on sexual experiences in childhood and concentrated, instead, on nonsexual, frightening events.

Modern Revisions of Psychoanalytic Theory

Since Freud's death in 1939, researchers have made tremendous advances in the understanding of normal and abnormal personality development. Two closely related schools of thought, object-relations theory and ego psychology, are presently revising Freudian theory to reflect this knowledge.

Object-Relations Theory Freud proposed that the infant is all id. Totally selfish, it lives almost exclusively for food. Though Freud wrote frequently about infancy and childhood, he based his ideas on adults' recollections. He had little real contact with children, even his own. And Freud discounted the role of the mother, except as a source of food and physical care. He later admitted that he had overemphasized the importance of the father and minimized the role of the mother because his own patients had cast him in the role of a male parent and consequently had revealed much more about their relationships with their fathers. More recently, female psychoanalysts such as Melanie Klein of the British Psychoanalytical Society have been able to discover much more about patients' feelings for their mothers.

Object-relations researchers took the obvious step of actually observing infants. What they found was that infants live in a close, emotional relationship with their parents, especially the mother. This appreciation of the interactions between mother and child, however, brought the researchers into direct conflict with Freud's description of the infant. In order for the child to have this sort of social relationship with the mother, it must have an ego from the moment of birth. This revelation opened the way for a whole new conceptualization of early personality development.

When a baby is born, it has a very limited understanding of the world. In fact, an infant does not even understand that objects have an existence separate from itself. It does not realize that the world is divided into two parts: itself and everything else. For example, to a baby, dream experiences are as real as conscious experiences, and its mother's hand is viewed as the same as its own. Because of this, many infants will grab the mother's hand, or suck the mother's thumb much as they would their own. Gradually, the baby comes to learn that it is physically distinct from other objects. It can control the movement of its own hand, whereas the mother's hand has a will of its own.

In a similar manner, the baby is psychologically indistinct from others at first. The development of the child's psychological independence parallels its sense of physical independence, but it takes much longer. A child of one or two acts as if his or her own thoughts and feelings are shared by all people and objects in the world. The child assumes that an adult or an animal knows what he or she is thinking. Even later, the child is unable to take the perspective of another person. This is illustrated in a conversation that psychologist John Nash had with a six-year-old named Pippa and recorded in his 1970 book *Developmental Psychology; A Psychobiological Approach*. "Pippa, what is your sister's name?" Dr. Nash asked. "Heather." "And who is Heather's sister?" "Heather hasn't got a sister." "But who are you, then? Aren't you Heather's sister?" "No, I'm Pippa."

As parents watch their child grow and develop, and help to shape its personality, they naturally come to assume that they know and understand the child fully. By adolescence, however, the child is completing the process of developing a separate psychological identity. Object-relations theory therefore has special implications for the family strife that often occurs at this stage.

The parents' understanding of the adolescent's personality and the adolescent's picture of him- or herself are different, and it is often the parents who are mistaken. Their image of the adolescent is outmoded, based on what their child has been in the past rather than what he or she has become. Instead of being a product of the parents' personalities and therefore completely knowable, the adolescent has become a distinct person, and therefore is as complex and unknowable as any other adult. Naturally this difference of opinion about the child's true self causes a lot of conflict. The only solution for the adolescent is to break away psychologically from the parents. If all goes well, the adolescent will realize that he or she is not rejecting the parents themselves, but rather the parents' image of him or her.

Of course, often the parents try to resist the growing independence of their child. If, however, the teenager accepts the parents' image of him- or herself, he or she may never achieve psychological independence. It is not unusual to encounter, for example, a 35-year old man who still lives with his mother and defines himself in her terms.

The next stage in maturity is for the adolescent to recognize that he or she is also independent of his or her peer group. This is not to say that the adolescent must strive to be different from them, only that his or her acceptance of their standards and values becomes conscious and voluntary rather than seeming like the only possible way of behaving.

Ego Psychology The theory of the three-part personality, consisting of the id, ego, and superego, was developed by Freud very late in his life. The ego psychologists, led by Freud's daughter, Anna, saw themselves as extending the theory in a direction Freud himself would have taken if he had lived long enough. The ego, in addition to its function as a mediator of the conflicts between the id and superego, is now seen as often functioning independently of this conflict. It is this part of the personality that perceives, understands, learns, and deals with the outside world. In therapy, according to this view, the analyst teams up with the healthy portions of the patient's ego in order to fight against the neurotic symptoms.

Freud and his disciples lived in a Europe ravaged by horrible wars, and they had witnessed the brutality of the Nazis. It was not surprising, then, that they had developed a pessimistic view of human nature in which life was a struggle to restrain the irrational demands of the id and to overcome the traumas of childhood. Ego psychology, with its emphasis on the emotionally healthy adolescent and adult, paints a more optimistic, future-oriented picture. As a result, many American analysts have enthusiastically adopted this viewpoint.

Probably the best-known writer among the ego psychologists was the Dane Erik Erikson. Born in Germany, Erikson never knew his father—his parents were separated before he was born. As a young man, he was acutely conscious of this lack of family identity. (As a child, he had used his stepfather's last name as

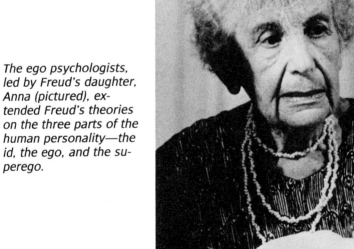

The ego psychologists, led by Freud's daughter, Anna (pictured), extended Freud's theories on the three parts of the human personality—the id, the ego, and the superego.

his own.) At the age of 37, he decided to become his own father, and adopted a new name to symbolize that he was Erik, Erik's son. Hence, he chose the name Erik Erikson.

In his psychoanalytic writing as well as his own life, Erikson expressed his belief that it was possible for an adult to grow and change. For Freud, personality had been essentially fixed by adolescence. Erikson extended Freud's concept of developmental stages throughout the life span, from birth to old age. He believed that people encounter crucial conflicts at certain times of their lives, conflicts that must be resolved if they are to continue their healthy development. For example, teenagers must try out many different roles, yet piece together a unified sense of their own individuality. Once they have become comfortable with their sense of identity, young adults can then face the challenge of developing mature relationships with others.

•   •   •   •

CHAPTER 7

HUMANISTIC AND RATIONAL THERAPIES

Humanistic and rational therapists stress strong self-concept as the basis of good mental health.

A theory as powerful and controversial as psychoanalysis was bound to provoke reactions. Psychoanalytic theory gives the impression that all people are helpless victims of forces beyond their control. Not surprisingly, many later philosophers and psychologists were disturbed by this picture of a passive human race whose chief goal seemed to be to avoid anxiety.

Instead, such theorists as Carl Rogers and Albert Ellis believed that each person's reality, and thus his or her behavior, is determined by a unique perception of the world. They felt that in order to understand a person's behavior it is necessary to view the world through that person's eyes. Several different theories of human nature have been proposed to express this viewpoint. Among them are humanistic psychology and rational-emotive therapy.

HUMANISTIC PSYCHOLOGY

According to Carl Rogers, humans are basically good, honest, and trustworthy, and their behavior is (or should be) motivated by positive strivings. Almost from birth, humans express curiosity and creativity, and they can experience a sense of joy from self-expression and personal growth. Rogers believed that life is a journey toward the full use of a person's abilities in productive achievements. People choose the paths they believe will lead them to this goal of self-fulfillment. Sometimes a person strays onto the wrong path—which is not so bad if the person recognizes the error. Many people, however, distort their perceptions of the

American psychologist Carl Rogers believed that life is a journey toward the full use of a person's abilities through productive achievement.

world to convince themselves of the rightness of their choice of paths. Anxiety, unhappiness, and neurotic symptoms occur, Rogers believed, when a person's internal perception of reality no longer matches his or her external reality.

As people mature, they develop a "self-concept," an image of what and who they are. A person with a healthy self-concept is confident of his or her abilities and assets, but knows his or her own limits. However, sometimes a person's developing sense of self is sidetracked or distorted. This most often occurs, according to Rogers, when parents set conditions on their love. For example, if a child misbehaves, does not get good enough grades, or disappoints the parent in some other small way, the parent may respond in a cold and rejecting manner. This "withdrawal of love" as punishment can be very harmful. Children who experience it learn that they are not worth loving for their own sake, but can only be loved when certain conditions are met. As in the Freudian superego, these conditions are unreasonable ideals of perfection. These children therefore learn not to love themselves unless they are perfect. Of course, no one is perfect, so children raised under these conditions cannot love themselves.

People who do not love themselves are especially vulnerable to threats to their self-concept from outside sources. Everyone can cite examples of people denying or minimizing blows to the ego. Sometimes bizarre distortions of reality may be required to maintain an inaccurate self-image. The person then accepts the distorted ideas as reality. This is what occurs in a psychotic, according to Rogers. The threatened self-concept not only gives the person a false picture of the world but also becomes stiff and inflexible in an attempt to protect itself. This is revealed in an inability to deal with trivial day-to-day setbacks.

Interestingly, Rogers believed that one's self-concept can also be threatened by unexpected positive events. He believed that one of the most important goals in a person's journey toward self-fulfillment is the confirmation of his or her self-image. If a person discovers that his or her sense of self is incorrect, it shakes the very foundations of his or her mental functioning. To protect this self-image the person may do something to reinforce it—despite the fact that it is negative. In this way, the person performs an act of self-preservation. According to Rogers, this confirmation of one's opinion of oneself is safe, familiar, and therefore comforting, despite the social harm it does. Freud, on the other hand, might say that the person acted self-destructively to punish him- or herself, to atone for some unconscious guilt. Rogers would say that the harm was an accidental by-product of a very important psychological goal: to confirm the self-image.

Rogers's Client-Centered Therapy

Based on his theory of the importance of the self-concept, Rogers developed client-centered therapy. The goal of this approach is to soften the client's stiff, inflexible self-concept and allow it to be more responsive to reality. The therapist encourages this by accepting and confirming the client's own subjective experience. By receiving from the therapist the "unconditional positive regard" (that is, affection and approval with no strings attached) that the client did not experience as a child, the client learns that he or she can love him- or herself under any circumstances. The therapist does not push or pull the client toward change, but only provides an accepting, undemanding environment in which change can occur. The client's natural tendency to strive for self-improvement does the rest.

Rogers believed that the solution to a person's problems had to come from within the self. He therefore rejected the conventional teaching that counselors should guide a person through the problems of the world. In fact, client-centered therapists go to the opposite extreme. The therapy consists largely of reflecting back whatever the client says. This is done by simply rephrasing the client's comments in a milder way so as to help the client learn what he or she is really saying and to confirm his or her view of the world.

An Evaluation of Client-Centered Therapy

Rogers was a scientifically oriented psychologist, and believed that his theory and methods should be subjected to careful testing. A great deal of research has indeed shown that providing a warm, supportive environment for the client encourages positive change.

However, many aspects of the theory disturb critics. Because client-centered therapy emphasizes the client's conscious, sub-

Dr. Albert Ellis believed that thinking and feeling are very closely linked. In light of this belief, he developed rational-emotive therapy.

jective experiences, many therapists feel that it ignores the influence of the past and the unconscious. Also, reflecting Rogers's belief in the trustworthiness of human nature, the method takes the client's reports at face value. This assumes that people are willing and able to describe their feelings and their perceptions of reality accurately. Much research has shown that people's self-reports are highly distorted, and that people often do not know what is actually happening inside their own heads.

There are also several practical problems in engaging in client-centered therapy. The therapist is so passive that many clients find the sessions confusing and unproductive. Also, like psychoanalysis, the therapy depends on a great deal of talking. Many people with problems are simply unable to articulate their feelings adequately. And finally, the method does not seem to work with the severely disturbed. These people do not have sufficient insight into either their own subjective reality or the world's reality to bring the two closer together.

RATIONAL-EMOTIVE THERAPY

Albert Ellis, the creator of rational-emotive therapy, began his career as a psychoanalytically trained psychologist. He became disillusioned with analysis, however, and began to develop a technique that would change his patients' behavior more quickly. The result of his research, rational-emotive therapy (RET), could hardly be more different from psychoanalysis.

Ellis's approach stemmed from his theory that thinking and feeling are very closely linked. Control over emotions can only be accomplished through controlling one's thoughts. According to Ellis, an event, such as failing to get accepted into college, does not directly cause depression, anxiety, or anger. The actual cause, he believes, is the person's thoughts about the event. RET teaches that most emotionally disturbed people are unrealistic thinkers. Not only do they wish to be successful, happy, and loved, but they demand it. They want to be perfect. Consequently, they fear and avoid the normal troubles and setbacks of life, which to them are devastating.

Ellis believes that changing one's behavior requires a lot of hard work and practice. In his therapy he attacks, criticizes, argues, and curses at patients in order to convince them that their thinking is irrational. To show clients that nothing horrible will happen to them if they radically change their behavior, Ellis has them do "homework assignments." A shy young man, for example, may be required to walk up to the next attractive woman he sees and ask her for a date. Another client might be told to give a speech on a crowded street corner. Once clients discover that their fears of looking foolish are exaggerated, they begin to realize that much of their behavior is based on false assumptions.

RET therapists attempt to replace their patients' irrational beliefs with rational ones. Patients are taught, for example, that there is nothing horrible in not being loved by everyone. True self-respect does not come from the approval of others, they say, but rather from liking themselves and doing what makes them happy. RET therefore emphasizes rationality, individualism, and self-sufficiency.

RET has always been controversial. Critics say that its techniques are stressful and dehumanizing. Ellis, however, argues that successful therapy must always involve some pain, but the quicker the client deals with the problem, the better. Many therapists agree with this explanation. In 1982, Darrell Smith of Texas A & M University conducted a survey of 800 clinical and counseling psychologists. The survey showed that Ellis was ranked the second most influential psychotherapist; Carl Rogers placed first and Sigmund Freud third. Although RET is certainly not meant for everyone and not every patient is comfortable with this type of therapy, it has helped thousands of people quickly alter maladaptive habits of thinking and behaving.

• • • •

CHAPTER 8

BEHAVIOR THERAPY

Ivan Pavlov, his assistants, and his dog.

A nine-month-old baby boy was starving himself to death. As soon as he was given food, even through a tube, he would vomit it back up. His weight had declined over a period of 4 months to 12 pounds. His skin hung in empty wrinkles over an emaciated body. Drugs, dietary changes, and loving nursing care had no effect.

As a last resort, doctors attached electrodes to his calf. Every time he began to vomit he was punished by painful shocks administered to his leg. Within a day, the regurgitation had virtually ceased. After 13 days of treatment, the infant's weight increased by 26%. Eight weeks later, he was a healthy, thriving child.

Behavior therapists believe that building up self-esteem or delving into the subconscious is a waste of time—instead, they feel that only the client's behavior is important, and that behavior can be modified through reward and punishment. Behaviorists do not explore the feelings of a client claiming to be lonely. Instead, the therapist will attempt to change the client's behaviors so that he or she will no longer lack companionship.

More than any other therapy, the behavioral approach owes its existence to psychological research, especially the study of learning processes called behaviorism. Behaviorists believe that practically all human behaviors are learned, including the behaviors called "neurotic symptoms." According to Gregory A. Kimble, Norman Garmezy, and Edward Zigler, authors of the textbook *Principles of General Psychology*, a prominent researcher in the field once said, "There is no neurosis that underlies a symptom, but only the symptom itself. Get rid of the symptom and you have eliminated the neurosis!" The symptoms, then, are merely bad habits that can be eliminated or replaced with more acceptable behaviors through means discovered in research on learning.

CLASSICAL CONDITIONING: RESEARCH AND THERAPIES

In 1895, Ivan Pavlov, a Russian physiologist studying salivation in dogs, discovered an interesting phenomenon. In order to stimulate the flow of saliva, an assistant would place a small amount of meat powder in a dog's mouth. Soon, the dog would begin drooling at the sight of the powder, and eventually at the sight of the assistant himself. Obviously, the dog had learned to associate the assistant with being fed. Exploring this phenomenon, Pavlov discovered that if a bell was rung when the meat powder was in the dog's mouth, the dog later salivated just to the sound of the bell.

Pavlov devoted the next 36 years of his life to studying these "conditioned reflexes." Despite the obvious importance of his work to human behavior, Pavlov rejected any connection between his work and thinking, emotion, or even psychology. He insisted that learning processes were purely physiological. This point of view has been passed down to present-day learning theorists, along with the assumption that human learning is merely a more elaborate version of the conditioning that occurs in animals.

The Stimulus-Response Connection

According to theories of behaviorism, all classically conditioned behaviors are reflexes that grow out of a few simple automatic physiological responses. The classic example of this is Pavlov's dog: The taste of food (a stimulus) causes salivation (a response). What Pavlov discovered was that when a secondary stimulus, such as a bell, is repeatedly paired with a stimulus that produces a response, such as the meat powder, the new stimulus will come to cause the same response. For example, if a spider bites a person, he or she may come to associate the spider with pain. Each time the person sees a spider, he or she will react with fear, thinking of the pain the particular spider caused. In addition, the person may react with fear to objects that only resemble spiders, such as harmless bugs or even pictures of spiders—despite the fact that pictures can not hurt the person.

There does not have to be any logical or causal connection between the new stimulus and either the original stimulus or the response. Conditioning will occur with any stimulus that is paired with the original. Thus, Pavlov's dog salivated at the sound of a bell, despite the complete lack of any natural connection between ringing noises and saliva. Instead of a bell, Pavlov could have used a flashing light, a poke in the dog's ribs, or any other sensation that the dog would be sure to notice. This effect is a large part of behaviorism's explanation of anxiety disorders.

Anxiety disorders, put simply, are illnesses in which the person fears things he or she cannot understand or express, or fears something or someone for no rational reason. A woman, for example, may fear her husband will be hurt in a car crash, when there is no logical reason for believing so. Nonetheless, this woman may experience extreme anxiety each time her husband leaves in a car. If a person is afraid of spiders, one would assume that a spider once bit the person and consider the fear normal. If a person is afraid of telephones, however, he or she is thought to be phobic. According to behaviorists, both of these people have simply learned the response because the object was in some way present at the time.

Flooding Therapy

If all symptoms of anxiety are acquired through learning, it then follows that it should be possible to eliminate them or replace them with harmless behaviors, based on techniques also discovered by learning theorists. One such technique is called flooding, developed in 1957 by psychologist Thomas Stampfl, a professor at John Carroll University in Cleveland, Ohio. When a newly learned stimulus is presented over and over but is never again paired with the original stimulus, the learned response will usually fade away. Thus, if Pavlov's dog hears a bell rung frequently, the dog will soon stop drooling. Each time the bell is rung the response will be less and less, until it disappears.

Flooding refers to overwhelming the person's system with the stimulus so that the response simply tires out. Someone with a phobic fear of cats, for example, might be locked into a small room with dozens of them. Eventually, if the flooding is properly done, the fear and anxiety that the cats produce will diminish. Of course, several conditions must be met in order for the therapy to be successful; for instance, the cats must be very tame and docile. If the phobic were to be scratched by a cat, the treatment would only increase the fear. Also, there is the danger that panic could so overwhelm the person that serious emotional harm could result. For these reasons, flooding must take place in a controlled setting, under the careful monitoring of a professional.

A variation of flooding is called implosion. In many cases of phobia, it is not practical or safe to confront a person with the actual fear-producing stimulus. In implosion therapy, the client is asked to imagine the anxiety-producing object or event as fully, vividly, and strongly as possible. In one case, a student with a strong fear of taking tests was asked to imagine the worst possible situation: trembling, freezing up, being unable to write anything on the exam—disgrace and humiliation. After a half hour of this self-imposed panic, the student found that he could no longer feel the same emotion. He simply could not sustain the same high level of anxiety. With each repetition, the anxiety became less, until he was able to take an actual test without fear.

Systematic Desensitization

Classical conditioning research also led to the development of a therapeutic technique called systematic desensitization, developed in its current form during the late 1950s by psychiatrist Joseph Wolfe. During experiments conducted at the University of the Witwatersrand in South Africa, Wolfe demonstrated that animals would not learn contradictory responses to the same stimulus. For example, it is impossible to teach a dog both to stand up and to lie down at the same command. Systematic desensitization requires a careful exploration of the client's symptoms to develop an "anxiety hierarchy," a list of fear-producing situations ranging from minimal to extreme. In one case of school phobia, the hierarchy was found to be as follows: (1) middle-of-summer vacation, relaxing on the beach; (2) buying school supplies; (3) driving by the front of the school; (4) waking up on the first day of school; (5) entering school through main doors; (6) sitting in algebra class; (7) being called on in algebra class.

In therapy the client imagines the anxiety-arousing situation while feeling a response that is incompatible with anxiety. Relaxation is usually used as the incompatible response. First the client is trained to relax. This involves alternately tensing and relaxing the muscles while the therapist suggests relaxing images, such as floating in a warm swimming pool. Relaxation training may take several sessions. Then the client is asked to imagine the situation in the anxiety hierarchy that arouses the least fear (middle-of-summer vacation, in the example above) while continuing to relax.

Once the person has become desensitized to this situation, the next step in the hierarchy is imagined until that, too, is no longer threatening. This is continued, in slow and systematic steps, until the most frightening event (being called on in class) can be imagined while maintaining a state of deep relaxation. The steps are then often repeated in real life, always accompanied by the relaxation response. Dr. Robert Motta, a therapist and professor at Hofstra University on Long Island, New York, sometimes uses systematic desensitization to treat patients with a fear of flying. Motta, himself a licensed pilot, includes such activities as driving by the airport without stopping, watching planes land and take off from the observation deck, boarding a parked plane, and a short flight in his own aircraft.

OPERANT CONDITIONING

The classical conditioning described in the previous pages is a passive kind of learning—the conditioning happens to the animal or person. Operant conditioning, on the other hand, calls for the animal or person to instigate the action or "operate" on the environment, and then learn from the consequences of its behavior. All of operant conditioning is based on a very simple principle. Behavior followed by a reward will become stronger and more common, and behavior followed by punishment will diminish.

A person's rewards and punishments usually come directly or indirectly from their actions. For example, if a man mixes flour, eggs, butter, and sugar in the right way, he will be rewarded by a feeling of accomplishment and a delicious cake. If a woman buys a pair of shoes too hastily, however, she will be punished by painful feet. These logical connections, however, are not necessary for learning. In the same way that there need not be a natural relationship between a bell and salivation for classical conditioning to occur, people learn to increase or decrease their behaviors even if the consequences do not have any rational or intentional connection to the actions. According to behaviorists, this point is crucial to an understanding of disturbed behavior and its treatment.

In 1948, B. F. Skinner, the best known of the behaviorists, first described the phenomenon of "superstitious learning." During his experiments, Skinner tried feeding pigeons at random intervals—for example, at 1:00, 1:05, 1:18, 1:19, 1:31, and 1:50. He discovered that the pigeons would often act as if their actions had brought on the reward. If one pigeon happened to be circling to the left before food was dispensed, it would tend to repeat the action. This made the pigeon more likely to be circling to the left just before the next food pellet, which would reinforce the apparent effectiveness of its behavior. In time, dozens of pigeons "learned" that their completely useless behaviors brought them food.

Skinner believes that much maladaptive human behavior is superstitious and, in some cases, easy to identify. "I broke the chain in that chain letter, and sure enough, a month later something terrible happened." But often the superstitious connection is more subtle. An anxious person may "learn" that counting the spots on the ceiling every night will protect his or her mother from harm.

Learned helplessness is the opposite of superstitious learning. In the previous examples, people learned behaviors they should not have. In learned helplessness, they fail to learn when they should. Much like Pavlov and his experimental subjects, scientists first studied this effect in animals. If a dog is caged and given electric shocks, it will naturally try to escape. If it fails in all its attempts, it will learn that it is helpless to avoid the shocks and will simply lie down passively. Later, even if a means of escape becomes available, the dog will not discover it, because it no longer tries.

Learned helplessness can also occur in humans. A child with violent alcoholic parents may learn that his or her actions are unable to affect whether he or she is fawned over or slapped on any given night. The parents' actions are unpredictable. Studies have shown that children growing up in such environments have little confidence in their ability to make something of themselves. The children tend to believe that fate, conspiracies, or random events determine people's lives. They have learned that they are helpless in their confrontations with the world, and are likely to become depressed as a result.

Sometimes behaviors that are usually irrelevant or even harmful can have rewarding consequences in unusual or unhealthy situations. Many teachers are plagued with one or two students who disrupt the class. Often the teacher accidentally encourages the unwanted behavior by paying attention to it. Even a scolding can be rewarding for a child who needs human contact. In the case of the nine-month-old infant, the starvation was an accidental negative consequence of the rewards that the vomiting

Implosion therapy involves imagining the worst possible outcome of a scenario and then mentally reliving it. A student with a fear of taking tests, for example, would imagine fright and tension until the emotions and the scene no longer evokes any fear in him or her.

brought. The regurgitation began at a time of great stress in his family. His mother was temporarily disabled with a broken ankle, she was struggling with her own mother over how to care for the child, and she was fighting frequently with her husband. The infant learned that his vomiting brought his family together and directed attention toward himself, uniting them in their concern for his health.

Once established, operant behaviors resist fading away. This is because the action becomes rewarding in and of itself. For example, the infant learned that vomiting relieved his anxiety and made him feel better, and so continued this behavior even after he was removed from his family. On a more positive note, the child who starts violin lessons to please his parents may eventually love practicing.

Operant-Conditioning Therapies

Therapies based on the operant model are usually rather simple in concept, but may not be so simple to put into practice. In general, the goal of the therapist is to encourage healthy, productive actions while discouraging harmful ones. Positive reinforcement, for example, means rewarding the client's appropriate behavior. This requires that the "appropriate behavior" be precisely defined. It also requires the therapist to know what a particular person finds rewarding. One child may enjoy attention, for example, whereas another likes candy, and a third simply wants to be left alone.

Finally, the client must be in a situation in which his or her behavior is likely to be brought out; otherwise, it cannot be rewarded and no learning will take place. To encourage a certain behavior, therapists often "shape" the action. For example, to embolden an uncommunicative schizophrenic to engage in meaningful conversations with others, he or she might first be rewarded for making any noises. Once this behavior is common, rewards would be given for full words, then sentences, then coherent sentences.

In some cases, known as token economies, an entire institution such as a reform school or psychiatric ward participates in positive reinforcement. Tokens that can be exchanged for such privileges as extra food or staying up late can be earned by appropriate behavior. All staff members, including guards or orderlies, take part as therapists. They are carefully trained in what sorts of behaviors are to be rewarded by how many tokens.

Punishment is only effective in discouraging improper behaviors rather than encouraging proper ones. This point is often misunderstood by harried parents who punish a child for failing to clean up his or her room, for example. Failure to clean a room is not a behavior; it is the absence of a behavior. Rewarding the child when the room is cleaned is apt to be more effective. However, there are many specific actions that are harmful and undesirable, including the baby's vomiting, and these may be stamped out by punishment. Some common examples are those used in treatments to discourage smoking and drinking. A client may be given the drug disulfiram, commonly known as Antabuse, which is harmless unless alcohol is consumed; if the client drinks, he or she becomes nauseated.

Behavior therapies are not specific techniques but rather a collection of approaches based on learning theory. The therapist must custom design a treatment plan for each individual problem. In most cases, the client must be willing to subject him- or herself to an unusual degree of discomfort or self-discipline. Often this does not present a great problem, as the harmful behavior is causing so much distress or disruption in the first place.

People do not like to think of themselves as controlled by the same physiological reactions by which circus animals learn their tricks, and for decades other psychotherapists were doubtful that behaviorists could achieve lasting cures. But the evidence is now clear: Behavior therapy can be an effective therapy for neurotic and psychotic disorders, and may offer the best hope of helping a person suffering from these conditions to return to a normal life.

•   •   •   •

CHAPTER 9

. . . .

A REVOLUTION
IN TREATMENT:
DRUG THERAPY

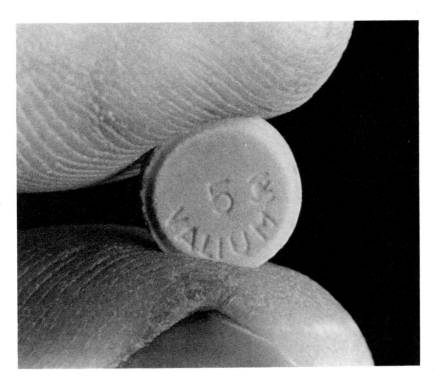

Valium.

Everything the mind does is a creation of the brain. One way to modify the workings of the mind, then, might be to alter the functions of the brain. The brain contains billions of neurons, or nerve cells. Each neuron receives information from hundreds or thousands of other neurons. The number of possible inter-connections among these nerve cells is therefore unimaginably large, yet each neuron performs just two basic tasks. First, the neuron transmits information to other neurons (or occasionally to other organs such as muscles or glands). Second, it combines and sorts out signals from other neurons. It may amplify and pass on some of the incoming signals or block others, thus making very simple "decisions." A person's thought process, therefore, is nothing more than enormously complex combinations of billions of these simple decisions. In order for these decisions to be made, however, certain chemicals found in the brain must first do their work. These chemicals, known as neurotransmitters, are responsible for transmitting messages from neuron to neuron.

Although the human brain is amazingly complex and fragile, it is also accurate and incredibly versatile in its functioning. Indeed, most of the brain's functions are completely unconscious and happen in the smallest fraction of a second. These processes are not so smooth, however, for some people. The neurotransmitters may not transmit—or may send messages incorrectly. As a result, that person suffers from a mental illness with biological causes, or perhaps one of the symptoms of the disorder has a biological cause. In any case, these symptoms, or the illness itself, can often be treated with psychoactive drugs.

Interestingly, psychoactive drugs do not directly affect the brain cells at all. Instead, they work by affecting the transmission of information from one neuron to the next. Neurons normally communicate with each other by transferring information across tiny gaps called synapses. This is done by a chemical action that happens when the first, or sending, neuron releases a neurotransmitter, which is sensed by the receiving neuron.

Psychoactive drugs alter the normal action of the neurotransmitters in a variety of ways. Some are chemically similar to the transmitter and "fool" the receiving neuron into responding as if it were receiving a burst of incoming messages. For example, the absence of the neurotransmitter dopamine causes Parkinson's disease, a disorder characterized by uncontrollable trembling. The drug L-dopa treats parkinsonism by causing neurons to react as if they had received dopamine. Other psychoactive drugs block the mechanism by which the receiving neuron recognizes its neurotransmitter, thus making it less responsive to incoming signals, much in the way anesthesia renders the body incapable of feeling pain. There are dozens of different types of neurotransmitters, and they perform different functions. Some

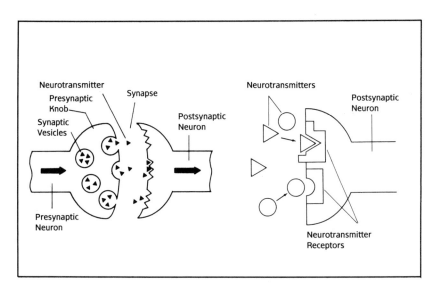

Neurons communicate with one another via neurotransmitters—chemical messengers that fit into receptors on the target neuron. Psychoactive drugs act as artificial neurotransmitters, often filling the receptors when a shortage of that particular chemical exists.

act as stimulants to the receiving neurons, speeding up their activity. Others act as depressants, slowing down the functions of the receiving neuron. But most important, different parts of the brain use different transmitters. It is possible to enhance or interfere with certain parts of the brain selectively.

Using drugs to affect the brain is certainly not new. Humans have always experimented with substances that have affected them psychologically. Alcohol is the most universal, but there are many others. Even the caffeine found in coffee, tea, and cola drinks has some influence on thinking. Many mentally ill people come to rely on drugs such as alcohol to numb themselves from the pain they are experiencing. Interestingly, according to psychiatrists Paul Wender and Donald Klein, authors of the book *Mind, Mood, and Medicine,* some depressed people also gain weight because they "medicate" themselves with sugar, which has a stimulant effect.

DRUGS FOR DEPRESSION

In the past, approximately 15% of patients who suffered from clinical depression or manic-depression committed suicide. Tragically, many of these deaths could have been avoided and the depression effectively treated with psychoactive drugs. Today, drug therapy saves tens of thousands of lives worldwide, as well as alleviating the suffering of hundreds of thousands more. Unfortunately, psychoactive drugs have problems as well, from unpleasant or even dangerous side effects to the agonies of addiction and overdose. The following list is comprised of drugs that are used legitimately, in a professional setting, for the treatment of specific mental disorders. None of these drugs should be used without a doctor's prescription and supervision, and without the presence of real illness. Used out of proper context, many of these drugs can be addictive. And they can be life threatening for a young person who experiments with any of them. For a professional, however, and for a person stricken with a debilitating mental illness, they offer hope for a productive, normal existence.

Monoamine Oxidase Inhibitors

The psychoactive effects of iproniazid, the first monoamine oxidase inhibitor, were discovered quite by accident. Iproniazid was originally introduced in the early 1950s to treat tuberculosis (TB). Physicians soon noticed that TB patients who were given the drug became euphoric. By 1956, doctors were using iproniazid to treat their schizophrenics and depressed patients. Although it failed to help schizophrenics, the drug dramatically alleviated the symptoms of depression.

Soon other drugs with similar actions were introduced, and it was proven that they had in common the inhibition of the enzyme monoamine oxidase (MAO). MAO normally neutralizes excess neurotransmitter molecules. By inhibiting over 90% of the activity of MAO, iproniazid and similar drugs allow certain stimulant transmitters to build up in quantity. Since these neurotransmitters are involved in the control of mood and general activity level, the patient feels more energetic and has a more positive outlook on life. Although these drugs are extremely effective in relieving depression, they are now seldom prescribed because of their dangerous side effects.

Many drug side effects occur because neurotransmitters or other psychoactive chemicals are used elsewhere in the body for other purposes. Since drugs circulate everywhere in the bloodstream, a psychoactive medication can throw other body chemistry systems out of balance.

Taking a dose of iproniazid and having a snack of wine and cheese, for example, can kill a person. This occurs because the enzyme MAO is also used in digestion. In particular, it breaks down tyramine, a common component of foods that can cause severe reactions if it accumulates in the blood. When these drugs are administered to control depression, the MAO in the digestive system is also inhibited, and the undigested tyramine can cause a sudden increase in blood pressure that can rupture blood vessels in the brain and cause death. To avoid this danger, the patient taking an MAO inhibitor must avoid eating anything that contains tyramine, including cheese, red wine, beer, pickles, and spoiled food.

Tricyclic Antidepressants

MAO inhibitors can also cause other side effects such as insomnia, fatigue, and fluctuating body temperature. Because of these problems, pharmaceutical companies raced to develop drugs that were as effective as the MAO inhibitors but did not have such dangerous side effects. Research focused on the drug imipramine, which had been shown by Swiss psychiatrist Roland Kuhn in 1956 to be effective in treating certain depressed patients. Those who complained of a loss of energy, including fatigue, inhibitions, and a slowing down of thought processes, for example, were greatly helped. The drug was not nearly as effective in patients with "agitated" depression, which often includes delusions. Imipramine was the first of the tricyclics, now sold under such trade names as Tofranil, Elavil, and Sinequan.

The tricyclics affect the same neurotransmitters as MAO inhibitors, but by a different mechanism. The MAO enzyme breaks down and "digests" many of the excess transmitter molecules, leaving others to be absorbed back into the sending neuron for recycling and later use. The tricyclics, however, appear to block this reabsorption, leaving the neurotransmitters in the synapse to continue stimulating the receiving neuron.

Different tricyclic drugs affect the neurons in slightly different ways. Some have a sedative effect on the patient, whereas others tend to energize. For reasons still unknown, both MAO inhibitors and tricyclics require between one and four weeks to begin to relieve symptoms.

Like most potent drugs, the tricyclics and MAO inhibitors are administered cautiously. The usual initial dosage is one pill each night at bedtime, unless the drug has a stimulant effect. The dosage is gradually increased, usually a little each week. When the patient's symptoms of depression begin to subside, the dosage is leveled off.

Lithium

In 1949, an Australian psychiatrist named John Cade published an article in the *Medical Journal of Australia* describing the remarkable effects of lithium, a natural salt, on a patient. Cade's subject was a man who had been in a state of manic excitement for five years. Within five days of treatment, however, his symptoms began to disappear. A few weeks later, still taking the drug,

A coffee taster examines coffee beans before they are roasted. Even drugs such as caffeine, found in coffee, tea, and soft drinks, can alter one's pattern of thought.

he returned to a normal, productive life. Other manics treated by Cade showed the same amazing recovery.

One would think that Cade's discovery would have caught the attention of the medical world. But it was not until 21 years later, in 1970, that the U.S. Food and Drug Administration (FDA) approved lithium carbonate as a prescription drug. This delay was partly due to Cade's being an obscure, independent researcher and in large part because of the economics of the drug industry. As psychiatrist Solomon Snyder explains in his book *Drugs and the Brain*, "The major antischizophrenic and antidepressant drugs, introduced to psychiatry in the mid-1950s, were all patented chemical entities. This means that each drug could only be sold by the firm that held the patent, guaranteeing considerable profit to the company in question." Lithium, being common and cheap, offered no such potential for profit.

Lithium, like the tricyclics and MAO inhibitors, has little effect on the mood of normal individuals, and is completely non-habit-forming. Lithium dosage, however, has to be very carefully regulated. Too small a dosage does not relieve symptoms, and too large a dosage may cause such side effects as kidney damage or goiter (an enlargement of the thyroid gland in the neck). A large overdose of lithium can be fatal.

Therefore, the concentration of the salt in the patient's bloodstream must be held within a narrow range. Doctors usually prescribe small doses of lithium to be taken several times a day, and they monitor the patient's blood concentration frequently. Blood tests are administered less frequently as the manic behavior disappears, and if the patient suffers no side effects, he or she can maintain the same dosage of lithium for years.

Despite a great deal of research, the reason for lithium's effect on mania remains a mystery. Surprisingly, lithium chloride has proved to have beneficial effects on depression as well. Somehow this chemical, closely related to common table salt, has the remarkable ability to stabilize mood.

DRUGS FOR SCHIZOPHRENIA

Like lithium, the first effective drug for treating schizophrenia was known long before its psychoactive properties were discovered. Phenothiazine was first synthesized in 1883, but it was not until 1934 that it was sold commercially—as an insecticide. In 1950, a related drug called chlorpromazine was developed in France. Within two years researchers discovered that this drug calmed agitated psychotics and reduced aggressiveness and delusions. Many schizophrenics regained contact with reality, to the great joy of their families and to the relief of their physicians. Later it was discovered that chlorpromazine had an additional ability: It could sometimes rouse withdrawn schizophrenics. This showed that the drug was not merely a sedative but actually affected the neurological causes of the disease. Over the years, many similar drugs have been developed and sold under such trade names as Thorazine, Compazine, and Mellaril.

The dosage required to reduce psychotic symptoms varies widely from patient to patient. Although most drugs are given in larger doses to heavier people (since such people have more blood, which dilutes the drug), this does not seem to be important for the antipsychotics. The severity of symptoms is also not a good predictor of the ideal dose. The only solution, then, is to administer a very small amount to the patient and wait to see if it has an effect. If not, the dosage is gradually increased. Once the proper level has been found, some patients experience very quick relief from the hallucinations and disordered thinking of schizophrenia, whereas for others, improvement is gradual.

The phenothiazine family of drugs appears to work by blocking the mechanism by which certain receptor neurons recognize their neurotransmitter. Normally the molecule of this particular neurotransmitter, called dopamine, fits into the receptor like a key turning in a lock. The antischizophrenic drug molecules, with shapes similar to dopamine, are like keys that fit into the lock but cannot be turned. They therefore prevent the real neurotransmitter molecules from entering, but they do not themselves have the stimulating effect of dopamine.

Most of the neurons that use dopamine as a transmitter are buried deep within the brain. This group of neurons controls two main aspects of psychological functioning. The first is the regulation of emotional behavior. Researchers now suspect that it is this function of the dopamine neurons that affects schizophrenic symptoms.

The second function of the dopamine neurons is to control areas of the brain responsible for coordinated movements of the arms and legs. If phenothiazines block the action of the dopamine neurotransmitter, it naturally follows that they should affect coordination as well. The principal side effects of these drugs are trembling and a lack of muscular coordination. (Remember that a lack of dopamine neurotransmitters is the cause of Parkinson's disease.) These effects are noticeable mainly during activities in which no conscious attention is paid to the muscles, such as walking or writing.

A more serious side effect appears after years of phenothiazine treatment. Apparently, the dopamine neurons that control smooth movement begin to compensate for the blocked receptors by growing new receptor sites. This produces an oversensitivity to stimulation in the facial muscles. A condition called tardive dyskinesia is the result; its symptoms include involuntary movements such as protruding the tongue, smacking and sucking the lips, frowning, grimacing, and grunting. Unfortunately, this condition, which can interfere with speaking, eating, and breathing, is often permanent, even after drug treatment stops.

DRUGS FOR ANXIETY

Humans have always attempted to relieve their anxieties through chemical means. Alcoholic beverages have always been used to relieve cares and dull sensitivity to both physical and psychological pain. Scientists developed a class of drugs called barbiturates around the turn of the century to produce the same effects. Barbiturates work by slowing down a wide variety of functions involving the central nervous system, including muscular movement, heartbeat, and thinking. In small doses, barbiturates act as sedatives, making one drowsy. In moderate doses, they put one to sleep. In large doses, they can cause death. Until the 1950s, physicians used the sedative effects of barbiturates to calm severely anxious patients. Phenobarbital, a mild but long-acting drug, was the most common type.

Barbiturates, however, remain extremely dangerous. They are highly addictive, and as with opiates such as heroin, patients develop a tolerance requiring larger and larger doses of the drug to produce the same effect. With opiates, the amount required for a fatal dose increases as the tolerance level increases. But with barbiturates, this does not happen: a longtime user who takes larger and larger amounts to achieve the same effect risks death with every dose. Barbiturates also interact strongly with alcohol; that is, each one accentuates the effect of the other. Taking ten drinks or ten "downers," as barbiturates are called, will impair physiological functions. But taking five drinks together with five downers can cause death. This is because both alcohol and barbiturates are depressants; they slow down the central nervous system. This slowing down, when amplified by both drugs and alcohol, can lead to respiratory failure and death.

Meprobamate and Benzodiazepine

Meprobamate, the first true tranquilizer, was developed through research on muscle-relaxing drugs. Introduced under the name Miltown in 1955, it almost instantly became the most commonly prescribed psychoactive drug. Research soon proved, however, that it had many of the same drawbacks as barbiturates.

Because Miltown sold so well, drug companies were inspired to search for a similar but safer drug. Scientists screened hundreds of chemical compounds until they found one formula that had the desired qualities. This drug, a benzodiazepine, had been created quite by accident and had been sitting around unnoticed in a laboratory for a year and a half. Research revealed that it alleviated worries and fears without causing sleepiness or dulling thought processes the way that barbiturates or meprobamate did. Now it was possible for a physician to prescribe a pill that relieved anxiety yet permitted the patient to drive safely and lead a normal life. When this drug was first sold under the trade name Librium in 1960, it marked a revolution in psychiatric treatment.

The different benzodiazepines are processed by the body at different rates, so doses vary according to the drug. Some must be taken several times a day, whereas others are effective when taken every other day.

Unlike antipsychotic drugs, tranquilizers seem not to affect the underlying causes of mental disturbance, but instead diminish anxiety from any source. Whereas antipsychotics have little effect on normal people, tranquilizers can relieve the everyday tensions that every person feels. Consequently, tranquilizers are more likely to be abused by those who do not really need them. In fact, up until the early 1980s, Valium was the most prescribed and most used drug in the United States.

Scientists are still unsure of exactly how benzodiazepines work, but they seem to make the receptor neurons more sensitive to a particular natural neurotransmitter called GABA. Because GABA depresses the receptor neuron, the drug acts to slow down the activity of those neurons that use GABA as their neurotransmitter. Not surprisingly, such neurons are found in parts of the brain that control emotions.

In some cases Librium and Valium cause drowsiness and drug dependence—yet in others they may offer freedom from the destructive effects of constant worry. As with any drug, however, they should be taken only for a diagnosed illness and under doctor's supervision.

COMBINING DRUGS AND THERAPY

Modern psychoactive drugs are so powerful and effective that an enormous burden of responsibility has been placed on the therapist who prescribes them. Serious scientific and moral questions have been raised about the ability of these drugs to alter mood and behavior. Do such drugs actually affect the mental illnesses, or do they merely mask the symptoms? With mania, depression, and schizophrenia, a case can be made that these drugs do indeed alter the disturbance itself. But this is probably not true of drugs that treat anxiety. Most clinicians regard anxiety as a symptom of a deeper disorder. If this is so, then is it ethical to prescribe drugs to relieve anxiety, or is the physician obligated to discover and treat the real underlying illness?

On the other hand, what about the therapist who is not a physician? If a psychologist or a counselor knows that a client's suffering can be relieved most quickly and effectively by drugs, should this therapist refuse to accept the client for a nondrug treatment? Mental health professionals are struggling with these and other difficult questions. One can only hope that they will always be resolved with the patient's best interests in mind.

A hundred years ago, a soldier who received a gunshot wound in the arm was likely to die from it. Smallpox killed millions of people; polio crippled more. Today medical science can readily treat the most life threatening of gunshot wounds, and smallpox and polio have been virtually eradicated with vaccines. Nevertheless, only since the 1950s have scientists made advances in psychotherapy, behavior therapy, and drug treatments to match those made in physical medicine. These therapies have rescued millions from disabling mental illnesses and suicide and offered hope for sufferers everywhere.

Conclusion

How can one possibly reconcile the theories of psychoanalysis and rational-emotive therapy, of client-centered therapy and behaviorism? How can the psychologist who interprets dreams and the physician who prescribes pills be treating the same problem? These views of human nature and of mental illness seem so contradictory that they could not all be right, but in a sense they all are. In the same way that a city is the buildings and streets it contains, the businesses and industries located there, and the people who inhabit it, a person is composed of many psychological parts, all of which are interconnected in an incredibly complex network.

•   •   •   •

APPENDIX:
FOR MORE INFORMATION

The following is a list of organizations and associations in the United States and Canada that can provide further information about mental illness.

GENERAL INFORMATION

American Mental Health
Foundation
2 East 86th Street
New York, NY 10028
(212) 737-9027

Canadian Mental Health
Association
2160 Yonge Street
Toronto, Ontario M4F2Z3
(416) 484-7750

Clarke Institute of Psychiatry
250 College Street
Toronto, Ontario M5T1R8
(416) 979-2221

National Alliance for Research on
Schizophrenia and the
Depressions
208 South La Salle Street
Suite 1428
Chicago, IL 60604
(312) 614-1666

National Alliance for the
Mentally Ill
2101 Wilson Boulevard
Suite 302
Arlington, VA 22201
(703) 524-7600

National Institute of Mental Health
Information Resources and
Inquiries Branch
5600 Fishers Lane, Room 15C05
Rockville, MD 20857
(301) 443-4515

National Mental Health Association
1021 Prince Street
Alexandria, VA 22314
(703) 684-7722

Office of Disease Prevention and
Health Promotion
National Health Information Center
P.O. Box 1133
Washington, DC 20013
(800) 336-4797
(301) 565-4167

AUTISM

Autism Services Center
Douglas Education Building
Tenth Avenue and Bruce Street
Huntington, WV 25701
(304) 525-8014
Hot line: (304) 525-8014

Autism Society Canada
20 College Street
Suite 2
Toronto, Ontario M5G1K2
(416) 924-4189

National Society for Children and
Adults with Autism
1234 Massachusetts Avenue, NW,
Suite 1017
Washington, DC 20005
(202) 783-0125

DEPRESSION

Depressives Anonymous: Recovery
from Depression
329 East 62nd Street
New York, NY 10021
(212) 689-2600

Manic Depressive Association of
Metropolitan Toronto
40 Orchard View Boulevard
Suite 252
Toronto, Ontario M4R1B9
(416) 486-8046

National Depressive and Manic-
Depressive Association
222 South Riverside Plaza,
Suite 2812
Chicago, IL 60606
(312) 993-0066

EATING DISORDERS

American Anorexia and Bulimia
Association
133 Cedar Lane
Teaneck, NJ 07666
(201) 836-1800

Anorexia Nervosa and Related
Eating Disorders
P.O. Box 5102
Eugene, OR 97405
(503) 344-1144

Glenbeigh Food Addictions
Hot Line
(800) 4A-BINGE

National Anorexic Aid Society
5796 Karl Road
Columbus, OH 43229
(614) 436-1112

National Association of Anorexia
Nervosa and Associated
Disorders
Box 7
Highland Park, IL 60035
(312) 831-3438

PHOBIAS

Concerned Agoraphobics Learning
to Live (CALL)
380 Tolosa Way
San Luis Obispo, CA 93401
(805) 543-3764

Freedom from Fear Foundation
Box 261
Etobicoke, Ontario M9C4V3
(416) 626-0603

Phobia Society of America
6000 Executive Boulevard,
Suite 200
Rockville, MD 20852
(301) 231-9350

Territorial Apprehension (TERRAP)
National Headquarters
648 Menlo Avenue
Menlo Park, CA 94025
(415) 329-1233

SCHIZOPHRENIA

American Schizophrenia
Association
Huxley Institute
900 North Federal Highway, #330
Boca Raton, FL 33432
(407) 393-6167
Hot line: (800) 847-3802

Canadian Friends of
Schizophrenics
Suite 309 at 95 Barber Greene
Road
Don Mills, Ontario M3C3E9
(416) 445-8204

SUICIDE

American Association of
  Suicidology
2459 South Ash Street
Denver, CO 80222
(303) 692-0985

Canadian Association on Suicide
  Prevention
c/o Dr. Antoon A. Leenaars
3366 Dandurand Boulevard

Windsor, Ontario N9E2E8
(519) 253-9377

Suicide Information and
  Education Center
Suite 201
1615 Tenth Avenue SW
Calgary, Alberta T3C0J7
(403) 245-3900
Crisis Phone: (403) 266-1605

To receive *Mental Health for Canadians: Striking a Balance*, a mental health promotion document, write:

Publications Division
Health Services and Promotion
  Branch
Health and Welfare Canada
Jeanne Mance Building
5th Floor
Ottawa, Ontario K1A1B4

STATE LISTINGS FOR DEPRESSION TREATMENT CENTERS AND SUICIDE PREVENTION CENTERS

The following is a list of local depression treatment centers and suicide prevention centers in the United States. The suicide prevention centers are available 24 hours a day and are certified by the American Association of Suicidology.

ALABAMA

Crisis Center of Jefferson County
3600 Eighth Avenue South
Birmingham, AL 35222
Crisis Phone: (205) 323-7777
Business Phone: (205) 323-7782

University of Alabama School of
  Medicine
University Station
Birmingham, AL 35294
(205) 934-2011

ALASKA

Fairbanks Crisis Clinic Foundation
P.O. Box 832
Fairbanks, AK 99707
Crisis Phone: (907) 452-4403
Business Phone: (907) 479-0166

ARIZONA

Southern Arizona Mental Health
  Center
1930 East Sixth Avenue
Tucson, AZ 85719
(602) 628-5221

ARKANSAS

University of Arkansas for Medical
  Sciences
4301 West Markham, Suite 506
Little Rock, AR 72205
(501) 661-5266

CALIFORNIA

Langley Porter Neuropsychiatric
  Institute
401 Parnassus Avenue
San Francisco, CA 94143
(415) 476-7478

Los Angeles Suicide Prevention
Center
1041 South Menlo
Los Angeles, CA 90006
Crisis Phone: (213) 381-5111
Business Phone: (213) 386-5111

University of California at
Los Angeles
Affective Disorders Clinic
760 Westwood Plaza-Box 18
Los Angeles, CA 90024
(213) 825-0764

COLORADO

Pueblo Suicide Prevention, Inc.
229 Colorado Avenue
Pueblo, CO 81004
Crisis Phone: (303) 544-1133
Business Phone: (303) 545-2477

University of Colorado Medical
Center
4200 East Ninth Avenue
Denver, CO 80220
(303) 394-8403

CONNECTICUT

The Wheeler Clinic, Inc.
Emergency Services
9 Northwest Drive
Plainville, CT 06062
Crisis Phone 1: (203) 747-3434
Crisis Phone 2: (203) 524-1182
Business Phone: (203) 747-6801

FLORIDA

Alucha County Crisis Center
730 North Waldo Road, Suite #100
Gainesville, FL 32601
Crisis Phone 1: (904) 376-4444
Crisis Phone 2: (904) 376-4445
Business Phone: (904) 372-3659

University of Miami Medical Center
Box 016960
Miami, FL 33101
(305) 674-2194

GEORGIA

Emory University School of
Medicine

Emory Outpatient Clinic
1365 Clifton Road NW
Atlanta, GA 30322
(404) 321-0111

HAWAII

University of Hawaii
Department of Psychiatry
1356 Lusitana Street
Honolulu, HI 96813
(808) 548-3420

ILLINOIS

Call for Help
Suicide & Crisis Intervention
Service
500 Wilshire Drive
Belleville, IL 62223
Crisis Phone: (618) 397-0963
Business Phone: (618) 397-0968

Rush Medical College
1720 West Polk Street
Chicago, IL 60612
(312) 942-5372

IOWA

Univerity of Iowa
Department of Psychiatry
500 Newton Road
Iowa City, IA 52242
(319) 353-3719

KANSAS

University of Kansas School of
Medicine
Department of Psychiatry
Kansas City, KS 67214
(913) 261-2647

KENTUCKY

Seven Counties Services
Crisis & Information Center
600 South Preston Street
Louisville, KY 40536
Crisis Phone: (502) 589-4313
Business Phone: (502) 583-3951

University of Kentucky
Department of Psychiatry
Kansas City, KS 67214
(606) 235-6005

LOUISIANA

Baton Rouge Crisis Intervention
  Center
P.O. Box 80738
Baton Rouge, LA 70898
Crisis Phone: (504) 924-3900
Business Phone: (504) 924-1595

Tulane Medical Center
Department of Psychiatry
1415 Tulane Avenue
New Orleans, LA 70112
(504) 588-5236

MARYLAND

Montgomery County Hotline
10920 Connecticut Avenue
Kensington, MD 20795
Crisis Phone: (301) 949-6603
Business Phone: (301) 949-1255

National Institute of Mental Health
9000 Rockville Pike
Building 10, Room 4S-239
Bethesda, MD 20892
(301) 496-5755

MASSACHUSETTS

Massachusetts Mental Health
  Center
74 Fenwood Road
Boston, MA 02115
(617) 731-2921

The Samaritans
500 Commonwealth Avenue
Boston, MA 02215
Crisis Phone: (617) 247-0220
Business Phone: (617) 536-2460

MICHIGAN

Suicide Prevention Center/Detroit
220 Bagley, Suite 626
Detroit, MI 48226
Crisis Phone: (313) 224-7000
Business Phone: (313) 963-7890

University Hospital
Department of Psychiatry
7500 East Medical Center Drive
Ann Arbor, MI 48109
(313) 763-9629

MINNESOTA

Crisis Intervention Center
Hennepin County Medical Center
701 Park Avenue South
Minneapolis, MN 55415
Crisis Phone: (612) 347-3161
Suicide Hotline: (612) 347-2222
Crisis Home Program:
  (612) 347-3170
Sexual Assault Service:
  (612) 347-5838
Business Phone: (612) 347-3100

University of Minnesota Medical
  School
Minneapolis, MN 55455
(612) 373-8869

MISSISSIPPI

University of Mississippi School of
  Medicine
Department of Psychiatry and
  Human Behavior
2500 North State Street
Jackson, MS 39216
(314) 362-2474

MISSOURI

Life Crisis Services, Inc.
1423 South Big Bend Boulevard
St. Louis, MO 63117
Crisis Phone: (314) 647-4357
Business Phone: (314) 647-3100

NEBRASKA

University of Nebraska
Nebraska Psychiatric Institute
602 South 45th Street
Omaha, NE 68106
(402) 572-2955

NEVADA

University of Nevada School of
  Medicine

Department of Psychiatry and
Behavioral Sciences
Reno, NV 89557
(702) 784-4917

NEW HAMPSHIRE

Center for Life Management
Salem Professional Park
44 Stiles Road
Salem, NH 03079
Crisis Phone: (603) 432-2253
Business Phone: (603) 893-3548

Dartmouth-Hitchcock Medical
Center
Community Mental Health Center
Hanover, NH 03755
(603) 646-5000, ext. 5855

NEW JERSEY

Fair Oaks Hospital
19 Prospect Street
Summit, NJ 07901
(201) 522-7000

NEW MEXICO

University of New Mexico School of
Medicine
Department of Psychiatry
2400 Tucker North East
Albuquerque, NM 87131
(505) 277-2223

NEW YORK

New York University Medical
Center
560 First Avenue
New York, NY 10016
(212) 240-5707

Suicide Prevention & Crisis Service
P.O. Box 312
Ithaca, NY 14850
Crisis Phone: (607) 272-1616
Business Phone: (607) 272-1505

University of Rochester
Department of Psychiatry
Affective Disorders Clinic
300 Crittenden Boulevard

Rochester, NY 14642
(716) 275-7818

NORTH CAROLINA

Suicide & Crisis Service/Alamance
County
P.O. Box 2573
Burlington, NC 27215
Crisis Phone: (919) 227-6220
Business Phone: (919) 228-1720

University of North Carolina School
of Medicine
Division of Health Affairs
Chapel Hill, NC 27514
(919) 966-1480

NORTH DAKOTA

University of North Dakota
Medical Education Center
1919 North Elm
Fargo, ND 58102
(701) 293-4113

OHIO

Central Psychiatric Clinic
3259 Elland Avenue
Mail Location 539
Cincinnati, OH 45267
(513) 872-5856

Support, Inc.
1361 West Market Street
Akron, OH 44313
Crisis Phone: (216) 434-9114
Business Phone: (216) 864-7743

OKLAHOMA

University of Oklahoma
Health Sciences Center and
Behavioral Sciences
Department of Psychiatry
P.O. Box 26901
Oklahoma City, OK 73190
(405) 271-5251

OREGON

Portland Division V.A.
3710 South West U.S. Veterans
Hospital Road
P.O. Box 1034

Portland, OR 97207
(503) 222-9221

PENNSYLVANIA

Contact Pittsburgh, Inc.
P.O. Box 30
Glenshaw, PA 15116
Crisis Phone: (412) 782-4023
Business Phone: (412) 487-7712

Medical College of Pennsylvania at
    Eastern Pennsylvania
Psychiatric Institute
3200 Henry Avenue
Philadelphia, PA 19129
(215) 597-7168

RHODE ISLAND

V.A. Hospital of Providence
Providence, RI 02908
(401) 273-7100

SOUTH CAROLINA

Medical University of South
    Carolina
Psychiatric Outpatient Department
171 Ashley Avenue
Charleston, SC 29425
(803) 792-4037

TENNESSEE

Crisis Intervention Center, Inc.
P.O. Box 120934
Nashville, TN 37212
Crisis Phone: (615) 244-7444
Business Phone: (615) 928-3359

Vanderbilt University
Department of Psychiatry
Nashville, TN 37232
(615) 322-4927

TEXAS

Suicide & Crisis Center
2808 Swiss Avenue
Dallas, TX 75204

Crisis Phone: (214) 828-1000
Business Phone: (214) 824-7020

University of Texas, Medical
    Branch
Department of Psychiatry and
    Behavioral Science
1200 Graves Building
Galveston, TX 77750
(409) 761-3901

UTAH

University of Utah
College of Medicine
Department of Psychiatry
50 North Medical Drive
Salt Lake City, UT 84132
(801) 581-4888

VIRGINIA

Eastern Virginia Medical School
Department of Psychiatry and
    Behavioral Sciences
P.O. Box 1980
Norfolk, VA 23501
(804) 446-5888

Northern Virginia Hotline
P.O. Box 187
Arlington, VA 22210
Crisis Phone: (703) 527-4077
Business Phone: (703) 522-4460

WASHINGTON

Crisis Clinic
1530 Eastlake East
Seattle, WA 98102
Crisis Phone: (206) 447-3222
Business Phone: (206) 447-3210

Harbor View Medical Center
Psychiatry Department
2H Harbor View Hall
325 Ninth Avenue
Seattle, WA 98104
(206) 223-3404

FURTHER READING

GENERAL INFORMATION

American Psychiatric Association. *Diagnostic and Statistical Manual of Mental Disorders: DSM-III-R.* 3rd ed., rev. Washington, DC: American Psychiatric Association, 1987.

Bird, Brian. *Talking with Patients.* 2nd ed. Philadelphia: Lippincott, 1973.

Cade, John F. J. "Lithium Salts in the Treatment of Psychotic Excitement." *Medical Journal of Australia* 2 (1949): 349–52.

Carlson, Dale. *Where's Your Head? Psychology for Teenagers.* New York: Atheneum, 1977.

Dinner, Sherry H. *Nothing to Be Ashamed Of: Growing Up with Mental Illness in Your Family.* New York: Lothrop, Lee & Shepard, 1989.

Good, William V., M.D., and Jefferson E. Nelson, M.D. *Psychiatry Made Ridiculously Simple.* Miami: Medmaster, 1984.

Kimble, Gregory A., Norman Garmezy, and Edward Zigler. *Principles of General Psychology.* 5th ed. New York: Wiley, 1980.

Looff, David H. *Getting to Know the Troubled Child.* Melbourne, FL: Robert E. Krieger, 1987.

Lubin, Bernard, et al., eds. *Family Therapy: A Bibliography.* Westport, CT: Greenwood, 1988.

Marks, Jane. *Help: A Guide to Counseling and Therapy Without a Hassle.* New York: Julian Messner, 1976.

Nash, John. *Developmental Psychology: A Psychobiological Approach.* Englewood Cliffs, NJ: Prentice-Hall, 1970.

Newton, Jennifer. *Preventing Mental Illness.* New York: Routledge & Kegan Paul, 1988.

Nicholi, Armand M., ed. *The New Harvard Guide to Psychiatry.* Cambridge: Belknap Press, 1988.

Pascal, Gerald R. *The Practical Art of Diagnostic Interviewing.* Belmont, CA: Wadsworth, 1983.

Rogers, Carl R. *On Becoming a Person*. Boston: Houghton Mifflin, 1961.

Snyder, Solomon H., M.D. *Madness and the Brain*. New York: McGraw-Hill, 1974.

Sue, David, et al. *Understanding Abnormal Behavior*. Boston: Houghton Mifflin, 1986.

Vinogradov, Sophia, and Irwin D. Yalom, eds. *Concise Guide to Group Psychotherapy*. Washington, DC: American Psychiatric Press, 1989.

Vonnegut, Mark. *The Eden Express*. New York: Praeger, 1975.

Wiener, Daniel N. *A Consumer's Guide to Psychotherapy*. New York: Hawthorne Books, 1975.

Yalom, Irving D. *The Theory and Practice of Group Psychotherapy*. New York: Basic Books, 1985.

AUTISM

Beavers, Dorothy Johnson. *Autism, Nightmare Without End*. Port Washington, NY: Ashley Books, 1982.

Lovaas, Ivar. *The Autistic Child: Language Development Through Behavior Modification*. New York: Halsted Press, 1977.

Paluszny, Mary J. *Autism: A Practical Guide for Parents and Professionals*. Syracuse, NY: Syracuse University Press, 1979.

DEPRESSION

Costello, Charles Gerard. *Anxiety and Depression: The Adaptive Emotions*. Montreal: McGill-Queen's University Press, 1976.

Greist, John R., M.D., and James Jefferson, M.D. *Depression and Its Treatment*. Washington, DC: American Psychiatric Press, 1984.

Hales, Dianne. *Depression*. New York: Chelsea House, 1989.

Klerman, Gerald L., ed. *Suicide and Depression Among Adolescents and Young Adults*. Washington, DC: American Psychiatric Press, 1984.

McCoy, Kathleen. *Coping with Teenage Depression*. New York: Signet, 1985.

Mackenzie, Richard. *Coping with Teenage Depression*. New York: New American Library, 1982.

Olshan, Neal H. *Depression*. New York: Watts, 1982.

Sturgeon, Wina. *Conquering Depression*. New York: Cornerstone Library, 1981.

DRUG TREATMENT

Byck, Robert, M.D. *Treating Mental Illness.* New York: Chelsea House, 1986.

Klein, D. F., R. Gittelman, F. Quittlin, and A. Rifkin. *Diagnosis and Drug Treatment of Psychiatric Disorders: Adults and Children.* 2nd ed. Baltimore: Williams & Wilkins, 1980.

Lickey, M. E. *Drugs for Mental Illness: A Revolution in Psychiatry.* New York: Freeman, 1983.

Snyder, Solomon H., M.D. *Drugs and the Brain.* New York: Scientific American Books, 1986.

Wender, Paul H., M.D., and Donald F. Klein, M.D. *Mind, Mood, and Medicine.* New York: Farrar, Straus & Giroux, 1981.

Young, Patrick. *Mental Disturbances.* New York: Chelsea House, 1986.

EATING DISORDERS

Bruch, Hilde. *Conversations with Anorexics.* Edited by Danita Czyzewski and Melanie A. Suhr. New York: Basic Books, 1988.

Brumberg, Joan Jacobs. *Fasting Girls: The Emergence of Anorexia Nervosa as a Modern Disease.* Cambridge: Harvard University Press, 1988.

Epstein, Rachel. *Eating Habits and Disorders.* New York: Chelsea House, 1989.

Erlanger, Ellen. *Eating Disorders: A Question and Answer Book About Anorexia Nervosa and Bulimia Nervosa.* Minneapolis: Lerner, 1988.

Garner, David, and Paul E. Garfinkel. *Handbook of Psychotherapy for Anorexia Nervosa and Bulimia.* New York: Guilford, 1985.

———. *The Role of Drug Treatments for Eating Disorders.* New York: Brunner-Mazel, 1987.

Halmi, Catherine A., J. R. Falk, and E. Schwartz. "Binge-Eating and Vomiting; A Survey of a College Population." *Psychological Medicine* 11 (1981): 697–706.

PHOBIAS

Agras, Stewart, M.D. *Panic: Facing Fears, Phobias and Anxiety.* New York: Freeman, 1985.

Doctor, Ronald M., and Ada P. Kahn. *The Encyclopedia of Phobias, Fears & Anxiety Disorders.* New York: Facts on File, 1989.

DuPont, Robert, ed. *Phobia: A Comprehensive Summary of Modern Treatments*. Rockville, MD: Phobia Society of America, 1983.

Goodwin, Donald W., M.D. *Phobia: The Facts*. New York: Oxford University Press, 1983.

Sheehan, David V., M.D. *The Anxiety Disease & How to Overcome It*. New York: Scribners, 1984.

Zane, Manvel, M.D., and Harry Milt. *Your Phobia: Understanding Your Fears Through Contextual Therapy*. Washington, DC: American Psychiatric Press, 1984.

SCHIZOPHRENIA

Bernheim, Kayla F., and Richard R. Lewine. *Schizophrenia: Symptoms, Causes, Treatments*. New York: Norton, 1979.

Dearth, Nona, Barbara J. Labenski, M. Elizabeth Mott, and Lillian M. Pellegrini. *Families Helping Families: Living with Schizophrenia*. New York: Norton, 1986.

Goodwin, Donald W., M.D., and Samuel B. Guze, M.D. *Psychiatric Diagnosis*. 3rd ed. New York: Oxford University Press, 1984.

Tsuang, Ming T., M.D. *Schizophrenia: The Facts*. New York: Oxford University Press, 1982.

Young, Patrick. *Schizophrenia*. New York: Chelsea House, 1988.

SUICIDE

Cain, Albert C., ed. *Survivors of Suicide*. Springfield, IL: Thomas, 1972.

Chiles, John, M.D. *Teenage Depression and Suicide*. New York: Chelsea House, 1986.

Fisher, Sheila A. *Suicide and Crisis Intervention: Survey and Guide to Services*. New York: Springer, 1973.

Hawton, Keith. *Suicide and Attempted Suicide Among Children and Adolescents*. Beverly Hills, CA: Sage Publications, 1986.

Hermes, Patricia. *Friends Are Like That*. San Diego: Harcourt Brace Jovanovich, 1987.

Hyde, Margaret O., and Elizabeth H. Forsyth. *Suicide: The Hidden Epidemic*. New York: Watts, 1986.

Leder, Jane Mersky. *Dead Serious: A Book for Teenagers About Teenage Suicide*. New York: Macmillan, 1987.

Leenaars, Antoon A. *Suicide Notes: Predictive Clues and Patterns*. New York: Human Sciences Press, 1988.

Lester, David. *Suicide from a Psychological Perspective*. Springfield, IL: Thomas, 1988.

Lester, David, Betty H. Sell, and Kenneth D. Sell. *Suicide: A Guide to Information Sources*. Detroit: Gale, 1980.

Shneidman, Edwin S. *Definition of Suicide*. New York: Wiley, 1985.

GLOSSARY

affective disorder mood disorder; mental disorder, the essential feature of which is a disturbance of mood manifested as full or partial mania, depression, or manic-depression

agoraphobia extreme fear of open spaces

amnesia loss of memory; usually selective and temporary, as in blocking out a traumatic event

anal stage in Freudian psychology, the second stage of sexual development, during which the child is concerned especially with his or her feces

anorexia nervosa an eating disorder characterized by an obsession with thinness and by loss of appetite; results in extreme weight loss

antipsychotic neuroleptic; class of drugs used to treat serious psychological disorders such as schizophrenia

anxiety an emotional state marked by restlessness, apprehension, and a sense of impending danger

anxiety disorder a neurotic disorder characterized by extreme anxiety and panic

autism a psychotic disorder characterized by a preoccupation with the inner world of thought and fantasy, often resulting in extreme detachment from anything outside of oneself

barbiturate a class of drugs used to slow down the central nervous system, acting as a sedative to both physical and psychological pain; infrequently prescribed because it is highly addictive and potentially fatal if combined with alcohol

behavioral therapy treatment of psychological disorders by modifying externalized behavior rather than by attempting to dislodge, understand, or treat mental and emotional states

bipolar disorder mood disorder characterized by the occurrence of one or more manic episodes; in almost all cases one or more major depressive periods will also occur

bulimia an eating disorder characterized by frequent binging and then purging of food

catatonia type of schizophrenia that manifests itself physically, either in wild, frenzied movement or in the assumption of bizarre, frozen postures

classical conditioning regularly evoking a certain response from a particular stimulus through training and repetition

client-centered therapy a method of therapy emphasizing the use of positive reinforcement to stimulate the patient's confidence and objectivity

clinical psychology psychology based on observation and the application and evaluation of objective and standardized testing

compulsion an irresistible impulse to behave irrationally, or the repetitive enactment of an irrational impulse

counseling professional aid in solving immediate problems that interfere with normal living

delusion false belief firmly held despite obvious proof to the contrary

depression as a mood: feelings of sadness, despair, and discouragement; as a disorder: a syndrome of associated symptoms, including decreased pleasure, slowed thinking, sadness, hopelessness, guilt, and disrupted sleeping and eating patterns

diagnosis the classification of an illness on the basis of its symptoms

displacement a defense or avoidance technique in which anxiety about or hostility toward one source is channeled to an innocent one

ego the personality component that, according to Freud, possesses consciousness and memory; mediates between instinctual needs and social reality

Electra complex a female child's sexual attraction to her father, accompanied by jealousy and hostility directed at her mother

fixation excessive attachment or preoccupation

genital stage in Freudian psychology, the stage of sexual development beginning with puberty, marked by an evolving sexual awareness of both oneself and others

hallucination hearing, seeing, smelling, tasting, or feeling things that are not there

hypochondria neurosis marked by obsession with one's health and imaginary physical ailments

hysteria disorder characterized by the conversion of anxiety into physical disability

id the part of the psyche that, according to Freud, possesses purely instinctual needs and drives

insanity legal term for a mental disorder in which the afflicted loses touch with reality and as a result is unable to distinguish between right and wrong

latency period in Freudian psychology, the stage of personality development lasting from age five until the onset of puberty, during which time sexual urges appear to lie dormant

libido energy associated with instinctual biological drives, such as the sex drive

lithium carbonate a crystalline salt used as a mood stabilizer in the treatment of manic-depression

mania a psychological state characterized by excitement, euphoria, rapid speech, flight of ideas, high energy, distractibility, irritability, and impaired judgment

manic-depression a mood disorder characterized by cyclical episodes of depression and mania

multiple personality disorder a hysterical neurosis in which an individual's personality becomes dissociated into two or more distinct personalities that alternately take control of his or her behavior; commonly confused with schizophrenia but in fact a separate illness

neurosis a mental or emotional disorder having no apparent physical cause, and in which the victim does not lose touch with reality

obsession a persistent idea, thought, impulse, or image that is intrusive and senseless, often resulting in compulsive behavior

obsessive-compulsive disorder a personality disorder characterized by an emotionally constricted manner in which one is preoccupied with rules, order, and organization to such a degree that normal social and occupational functioning are impaired

Oedipal complex a male child's sexual desire for his mother, accompanied by jealousy and hostility directed at his father

oral stage in Freudian psychology, the first stage of sexual development, lasting until approximately age two, in which the child derives gratification from use of the mouth in such activities as eating, sucking, biting, and crying

paranoia a psychosis characterized by delusions of persecution or of grandeur

pathology study of the causes and nature of a disease and of the changes in structure and function it may produce

personality disorder a mental disturbance in which personality traits are inflexible, maladaptive, and distorted, causing the afflicted both functional impairment and severe distress

phallic stage in Freudian psychology, the third stage of sexual development, lasting until about the age of five, in which a child is preoccupied with his or her genital organs

phenothiazine antipsychotic drug used in the treatment of schizophrenia

phobia a persistent, irrational fear

prognosis a prediction of the course and outcome of an illness

projection the attribution of one's own ideas or emotions to others in order to shift guilt or responsibility or to ward off anxiety

psychiatry branch of medicine dealing with the diagnosis and treatment of mental disorders

psychoactive drug drug affecting the mind or behavior

psychoanalysis a method of psychotherapy developed by Freud in which the doctor helps the patient recognize and release unconscious, repressed conflicts, feelings, and fixations

psychology the scientific study of normal and abnormal thought processes and emotions and their effects upon behavior

psychopath a person with a mental disorder manifesting itself in aggressive, antisocial behavior

psychosexual development evolution of the personality from birth to sexual maturity

psychosis a mental disturbance characterized by a loss of touch with reality

psychotherapy the treatment of mental disorders using techniques such as suggestion, persuasion, insight, reinforcement, and reeducation in order to alter maladaptive behavior and encourage personality growth

rational-emotive therapy (RET); therapy emphasizing rationality and self-sufficiency over emotionalism and self-indulgence

regression reversion to an earlier mental or behavioral level in response to stress and in order to avoid responsibility

schizophrenia mental disorder in which a person loses touch with reality; characterized by profound emotional withdrawal and bizarre behavior; often includes delusions and hallucinations

sociopath a person manifesting antisocial behavior or character traits

superego the part of the mind that, according to Freud, reflects the moral values and consciousness of authority and society

tranquilizer an antipsychotic drug used to calm or pacify

unipolar depression mood disorder characterized by one or more episodes of depression

INDEX

Allan Lundy holds a Ph.D. in social psychology from Harvard University. He served on the faculty of Hofstra University for seven years, teaching social psychology courses in the clinical and school psychology program and conducting research on social psychology and psychological testing. He has published articles in several scientific journals and has been a researcher for the Walter Reed Army Institute of Research in Washington, D.C. He is currently a visiting associate professor of psychology at Wesleyan University.

Solomon H. Snyder, M.D., is Distinguished Service Professor of Neuroscience, Pharmacology, and Psychiatry and director of the Department of Neuroscience at the Johns Hopkins University School of Medicine. He has served as president of the Society for Neuroscience and in 1978 received the Albert Lasker Award in Medical Research for his discovery of opiate receptors in the brain. Dr. Snyder is a member of the National Academy of Sciences and a Fellow of the American Academy of Arts and Sciences. He is the author of *Drugs and the Brain, Uses of Marijuana, Madness and the Brain, The Troubled Mind,* and *Biological Aspects of Mental Disorder.* He is also the general editor of Chelsea House's ENCYCLOPEDIA OF PSYCHOACTIVE DRUGS.

C. Everett Koop, M.D., Sc.D., is former Surgeon General, Deputy Assistant Secretary for Health, and Director of the Office of International Health of the U.S. Public Health Service. A pediatric surgeon with an international reputation, he was previously surgeon-in-chief of Children's Hospital of Philadelphia and professor of pediatric surgery and pediatrics at the University of Pennsylvania. Dr. Koop is the author of more than 175 articles and books on the practice of medicine. He has served as surgery editor of the *Journal of Clinical Pediatrics* and editor-in-chief of the *Journal of Pediatric Surgery,* Dr. Koop has received nine honorary degrees and numerous other awards, including the Denis Brown Gold Medal of the British Association of Paediatric Surgeons, the William E. Ladd Gold Medal of the American Academy of Pediatrics, and the Copernicus Medal of the Surgical Society of Poland. He is a Chevalier of the French Legion of Honor and a member of the Royal College of Surgeons, London.